Memories of the Robbie Doggie

"Robbie Lemkin, Freeze Dried"

By PHILLIP LEMKIN © 2011

I.S.B.N. 978-1-257-62394-5

MEMORIES OF THE ROBBIE DOGGIE

"Robbie Lemkin, Freeze Dried"

By PHILLIP LEMKIN © 2011

DEDICATION

This is NOT a "religious book", because religion controls, divides, intimidates and kills, but this book is dedicated to the creator of this universe, the One True God of Abraham, Isaac and Israel (Jacob), also known as YAHWEH, JHWH, JEHOVAH, YESHUA, Lion of the Tribe of JUDAH, & MORE.

You may know Him as Jesus of Nazareth, but He never used that Greek name, IESSOUS, for He was manifested in the flesh as a man-child in BEIT LEHEM (the House of Bread) in JUDEA, as the Son of David, KING of ISRAEL. He is the JEWISH MESSIAH (CHRISTOS in GREEK) of both Jew and Gentile & to HIM ALONE do I give the Glory of the gift of ROBBIE to our lives.

May the stories about our ROBBIE bring as much JOY, LOVE and PLEASURE to the readers as he enhanced our own lives for those wonderful years that he lived as part of our family.

"Memories of the Robbie Doggie"   ~~~   Robbie Lemkin, Freeze Dried

1 Nov. 1991 – 22 Oct. 2007

The title comes from what a little girl, named Amber, called my dog when we met while working at "Dr Stan's", together with the decision not to bury him on the day he left me. I give thanks to God for all the people Robbie touched during his most blessed life.

FRIENDS, CANINES, COUNTRYMEN, LEND ME YOUR EARS!

I have come to PRAISE ROBBIE, not to bury him.

The good that Robbie did lives after him………

(Apologies to Bill Shakespeare)

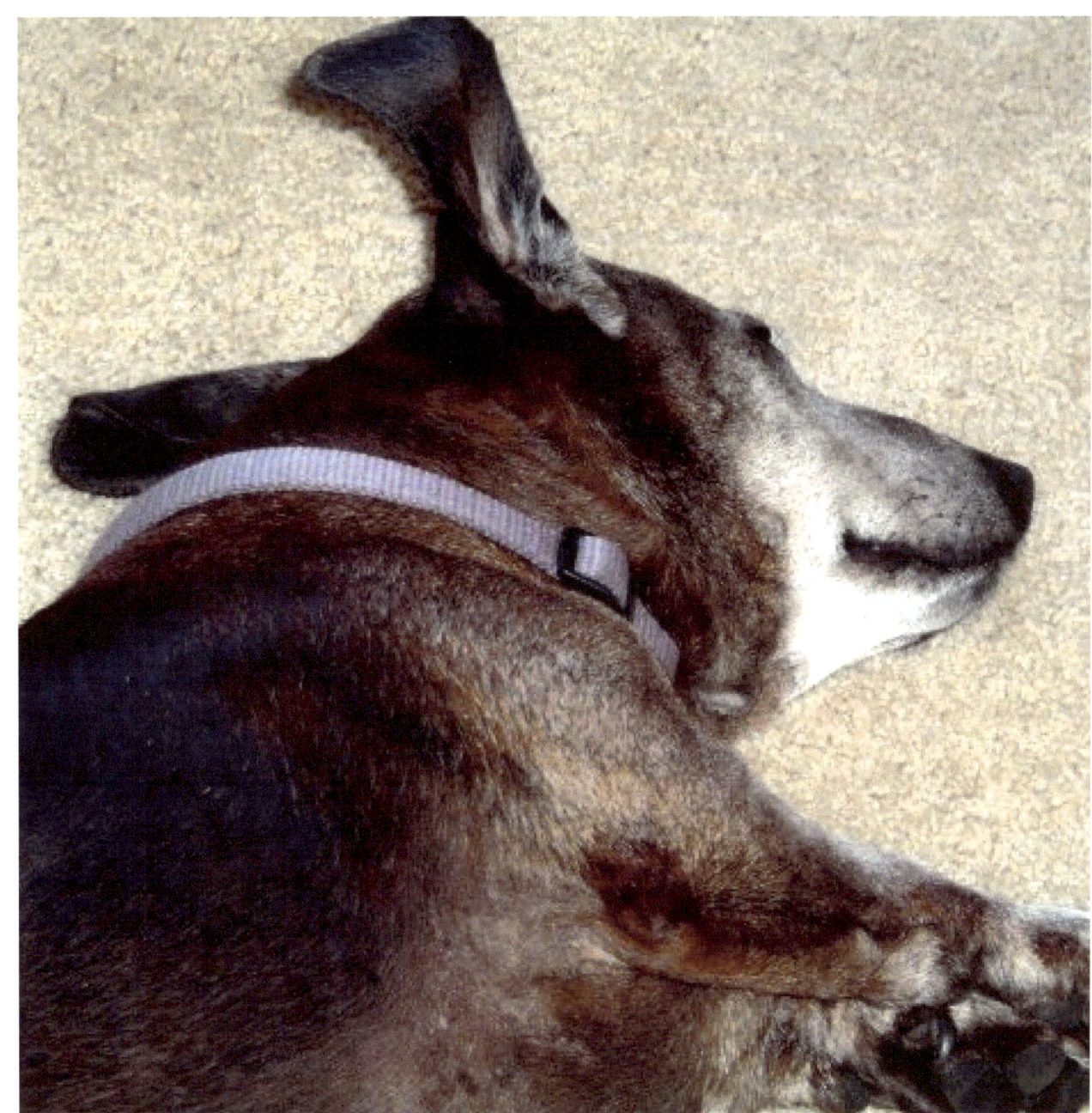

My three dogs were all full-sized dachshunds. When I was 8 yrs old, in 1951, dad brought home a 6 weeks old puppy that I named Karl, a black & tan, who became very obese and lived for only 8 ½ years. He had a pedigree, but dad bought him for only $A20.00 because he had a blemish on his navel and could not be shown.

I was unkind to him and he became more attached to my mother. How I regretted the way I treated Karl for many years afterwards. He was a very smart dog. He watched the way my dad; a true environmentalist, recycler before our time, emptied the kitchen scraps into the gardens and buried them in the soil, and you know he would do his business in the same gardens and cover it with his nose pushing the dirt over it. He hardly ever spoiled on the grass, which was good for I practiced my golf chip shots on our grass backyard, aiming at the small lemon tree plot in the far corner next to the gate to our neighbor doctor's hard tennis court.

Significance of Phillip's heritage as a Levite

My point here being that as a descendant of Levi, I have inherited the attributes, blessings and some of the negative aspects according to the prophesies of Moses and Jacob (Israel) concerning Levi"s descendants in the Last Days.
(See Genesis 49:5-7 & Deuteronomy 33:8-11)

Jacob said, "...Instruments of cruelty are in their habitations.....Cursed be their anger, for it was fierce: and their wrath, for it was cruel...."Although Moses later prophesied wonderful blessings upon Levi, there still remains this cruelty streak that must always be dealt with in any Levite. It may be in sharp, harsh words or even in bad reactions. It would explain why I acted badly towards my beloved dog, even as a young child who loved his dog. I remember several acts of cruelty that resulted in beatings from my father. I did not have a happy childhood. Because of the hardships in his own childhood, my father was not able to show his love towards me. It was no wonder that I took out my aggression upon my poor dog. I cried out to God for forgiveness for many years after Karl died.

Gate to tennis court at right

don't touch!

Karl at North Bondi in 1952 & 1953. (Australia)

PHILLIP, KARL, COUSIN KAYE

PHILLIP & 3 NEIGHBORS WITH PUPPY KARL (1951)

MY FAMILY HOME IN NORTH BONDI, SYDNEY

WE HAD A FORMER GRASS TENNIS COURT FOR OUR BACK YARD, (THAT WAS BUILT OVER A FORMER SWAMP) THAT SOON SUNK OUR IDEA OF HAVING A TENNIS COURT, THAT WAS MADE WHEN MY MOTHER'S FATHER, CHARLES MARKS, THE ONLY GRANDPARENT THAT I KNEW AS A CHILD, HAD BUILT OUR HOME IN 1938 WITH WINNINGS FROM THE STATE LOTTERY JUST TWO YEARS EARLIER. IT WAS A SPANISH BUNGALOW-STYLE HOME, ARCHITECT DESIGNED AND COSTING ABOUT $A1,200.00 IN 1936. THE SAME BUILDER HAD BUILT ANOTHER HOME 2 DOORS UP OUR STREET THAT WAS BUILT UPON A DOUBLE-SIZED BLOCK OF LAND. OUR NEIGHBOR WAS A "WAR BRIDE" MARRIED TO AN AMERICAN, AND HAD NO CHILDREN. THOSE WERE THE BEGINNING DAYS OF THE STATE LOTTERY, THAT WAS TO "PROVIDE FUNDING FOR THE HOSPITALS." MY PARENTS HAD SHARED A WINNING TICKET OF FIVE THOUSAND POUNDS ($A10,000) WITH ABOUT 8 OTHERS IN OUR FAMILY SO IN TODAY'S TERMS THAT $1,000 WAS MORE THAN ENOUGH TO BUILD A GRAND HOME.

It was a novelty and photo in the paper to win then, as Australia had no Social Security system in force after the effects of the Great Depression. Anyway, our family doctor whose hard, clay tennis court backed onto our fence was available for our use with a gate at the connecting fence. They would face a barking dachshund whenever they tried to retrieve tennis balls. He was o.k. if they did not try to get over the top of the fence. He bit their ankles if they jumped the fence. We used the high fences to grow vines like passion fruit and chocos around the three sides of our large gardens.

FAMILY HERITAGE

Although brought up as an Orthodox Jew, as I mentioned above, I am really a LEVITE, a Korathite son of Levi, of the high priestly family from the House of AARON. I believe and have been told by another Lemkin from New Jersey who migrated from Lithuania in 1955 that many of our ancestors were Rabbis in RIGA, LATVIA, where my father and mother's families migrated to Australia from, over 100 years ago. Their parents sailed from Europe via South Africa in 1902 & on to Australia in 1903. My father had an older sister, ROSE, and two younger brothers, Sol & Gus who were born in Murrurrundi, New South Wales, where my mother, Dorothy Mae Marks was born on Rosh Hashanah, 1904. My father's mother, MARY, and my mother's mother, MINNIE were SISTERS, from the family of MANDEL, which made me and my sister, Dawn, children from first cousins.

Long before we were born, my aunt Rose travelled to Tahiti on her honeymoon and never returned to her family in Australia. She migrated through Los Angeles from Tahiti and became an American, raising four wonderful daughters, Yvonne, Marilyn, Maxine and Mignon in Escondido, Ca.

God brought my cousin, Yvonne to Sydney in 1979 for our first family reunion since her mother, Rose left in 1927. There had been no contact since World War II. Although we were not listed in the Sydney telephone directory, Yvonne looked through all the State's phone books to find the lone Lemkin, my uncle Sol, on the central coast to get our number and 30 minutes later was on our doorstep, because it was only a 15 minute ride on the express train from the center of Sydney to Burwood.

Her sister, Mignon visited our home before and after I was born, as she was a nurse in the Pacific during W.W. II and was permitted to fly by helicopter from Brisbane down to Sydney twice that I know of. My parents told me she was with General Douglas MacArthur on R.& R. I next met her in Portland, Oregon in 1996 at her grand-daughter, Carla's wedding. Long after my parents had gone to be with the Lord, I found an old letter dated 1944 from my cousin Mignon to them commenting on how lovely I was as a baby.

We are a small family name, but one of my relatives, a Polish Canadian, named Raphael Lemkin, actually coined the word "Genocide" and was honored greatly by the United Nations after World War II.

Here is the article from the records of American Jewish Historical Society:

RAPHAEL LEMKIN
WAR DEPARTMENT IDENTIFICATION, 1946
RAPHAEL LEMKIN PAPERS, AJHS

Guide to the Raphael Lemkin (1900-1959) Collection, undated, [1763]-2002, (bulk 1941-1951)

P-154   Processed by Tanya Elder

American Jewish Historical Society

Center for Jewish History

15 West 16th Street

New York, NY 10011   Phone: (212) 294-6160   Fax: (212) 294-6161

Email: info@ajhs.org   URL: http://www.ajhs.org

© 2003. AMERICAN JEWISH HISTORICAL SOCIETY, NEWTON CENTRE, MA AND NEW YORK, NY. ALL RIGHTS RESERVED. CENTER FOR JEWISH HISTORY, PUBLISHER.

Descriptive Summary

Creator:	Lemkin, Raphael (1900-1959)
Title:	Raphael Lemkin Collection
Dates:	undated, [1763]-2002 (bulk 1941-1951)
Abstract:	<u>**Raphael Lemkin, an international lawyer, initiated the use of the term "genocide," and succeeded in persuading the United Nations to adopt the Genocide Convention in 1948.**</u> Documents include personal correspondence and artifacts; correspondence, documentation, clippings, and articles regarding the United Nations adoption of the Convention on the Prevention and Punishment on the Crime of Genocide treaty; and source material for the unfinished manuscript, HISTORY OF GENOCIDE. Collection includes photographs, identity cards, articles, papers, essays, clippings, magazines, research materials, term papers, posters, United Nations materials, and microfilm.
Languages:	The collection is in English, French, Hebrew, German, Polish, Russian, Spanish, Swedish, Norwegian, and Lithuanian.
Quantity:	12 manuscript boxes, 2 oversized boxes. 7.5 linear ft.
Identification:	P-154
Repository:	American Jewish Historical Society

Raphael Lemkin was born in Bezwodene, Poland (located in imperial Russia at the time of Lemkin's birth and now near Volkovysk, Belarus), on June 24, in 1900, though some sources claim 1901 as his birth year. 1 Little is known of Lemkin's early life in Poland, a point mentioned in the **only full-length biography written to date about Lemkin by Dr. James Martin, a Holocaust revisionist.** 2 What is known is that **Lemkin was one of three children born to Joseph and Bella (Pomerantz) Lemkin, all boys, including brothers Elias and Samuel.** According to various sources, **his father was a farmer and his mother a highly intellectual woman who was a painter, linguist, and philosophy student with a large collection of books in literature and history. With his mother as an influence,** <u>**Lemkin mastered nine languages by the age of 14, including English, French, Spanish, Hebrew, Yiddish, and Russian.**</u> At the age of 15, Lemkin first encountered the idea of intentional mass murder of a population when ==news of the Turkish slaughter of Armenians reached Poland in 1915.== 3 In addition, the novel QUO VADIS, **by the Polish author Henryk Sienkiewicz, describing the barbarity of the Roman Empire under Nero, is cited as an additional influence on the young, sensitive, and impressionable Lemkin. Later in life, the** ==1933 slaughter of Christian Assyrians in Iraq propelled his work on the legal concepts of mass murder.==

In 1919, he began the study of linguistics at the University of John Casimir in Lwow (Lvov, Poland), moved on to the University of Heidelberg in Germany to study philosophy, and returned to Lwow to study law at John Casimir in 1926, becoming a prosecutor in Warsaw at graduation. From 1929-1934, Lemkin was the Public Prosecutor for the district court of Warsaw. While Public Prosecutor, he wrote books on the law and worked on the team that codified the penal codes of Poland, which had gained independence from Russia in 1917. An important contact in the United States was forged during this time, when Lemkin worked with visiting Duke University law professor, Malcolm McDermott, in translating the THE POLISH PENAL CODE OF 1932. McDermott would later provide Lemkin with help in leaving Europe.

In 1933, as public prosecutor, Lemkin presented a paper at the Madrid meeting of the **League of Nations**, urging the delegation to condemn acts of vandalism and barbarity as crimes against humanity. He proposed, prior to creating an actual word for it, that the "destruction of national, religious, and racial groups" should be declared "an international crime alongside piracy, slavery, and drug smuggling." He proposed a ban on mass slaughter, but could not persuade the League to vote on it, with the Nazi delegation laughing at the idea of such a proposal. The presentation of his ideas at the League of Nations proved to be detrimental to his career as lead prosecutor, though being Jewish in Poland added to his career decline. Shortly after the Madrid meeting, he was admonished by the Polish Foreign Minister and under pressure, resigned his position in 1934, going into private practice until 1939.

When Germany invaded Poland in 1939, Lemkin joined the underground guerilla movement in the forests of Poland. After spending six months avoiding the Germans and making his way to Lithuania, he escaped to Sweden. In Sweden from 1940-1941, he was a lecturer at the University of Stockholm, presenting a series of lectures on international finance, published under the title VALUTAREGLERING OCH CLEARING (EXCHANGE CONTROL AND CLEARING), while persuading Swedish officials to provide him with copies of Nazi directives issued to occupied countries. Professor McDermott invited Lemkin to join him at Duke in North Carolina, and with the Nazi directives in hand, he made an arduous eastern journey through Russia and Japan, arriving on the East coast of the U.S. in 1941. In the U.S., Lemkin presented the confiscated Nazi directives to the State and War Departments, and began lecturing at Duke.

At the outbreak of American participation in the war, the U.S. Army recruited Lemkin to teach classes in military government while the Board of Economic Warfare gave him a position as a consultant due to his work on international finance law. From 1941-1943, he worked on his most well known publication, AXIS RULE IN OCCUPIED EUROPE, in which he continued his work on the 1933 Madrid proposal, published the translated Nazi directives obtained in Sweden, analyzed Axis authority and policies in occupied Europe, and introduced the term and concept of genocide. Chapter 9 of AXIS RULE developed Lemkin's theories on genocide, the word being a combination of the Greek "genos" or "race" and the Latin "cide" or "killing," thus forming a new concept of killing based on the deliberate destruction of a national, racial, ethnic, religious, or political minority by the majority or dominating society.

At the end of the war, the great majority of Lemkin's European family had died. His brother Elias survived with his wife and two sons. Raphael and Elias had a brief reunion in Europe, and Elias wrote letters from a U.S.-controlled Munich repatriation camp to Lemkin asking for help in immigrating to Canada, where additional Lemkin family were located in Montreal and Ottawa. From correspondence in the collection, Elias and his family successfully left Europe for Montreal in 1948.

In 1945-1946, Lemkin left his paid position with the Army, moving on to become an advisor to the U.S. Supreme Court Justice and Nuremberg Trial Judge, Robert Jackson. During the trials, he fought to have the word genocide introduced into the trial record, but his efforts were unsuccessful. British prosecutors objected on the grounds that the word was not found in the OXFORD ENGLISH DICTIONARY.

After Nuremberg, Lemkin turned to the United Nations General Assembly convened at Lake Success, NY in an effort to have the newly formed body condemn the act of genocide as an international standard. Lemkin presented a draft resolution for a Genocide Convention treaty to the countries of Cuba, India, and Panama, persuading them to sponsor the resolution. With the support of the United States, the resolution was placed before the General Assembly for consideration, with the various arguments and legalities over the document debated in the Legal Committee and the Social and Economic Council. The final draft of Resolution 96 (I) was presented to and approved by the General Assembly on December 11, 1946. The resolution affirmed that genocide was a crime under international law and directed the Member States and the Social and Economic Council to draft a treaty to present to Member States for ratification.

From 1947-1948, the Convention on the Prevention and Punishment on the Crime of Genocide treaty was hashed out with Lemkin regularly consulting on the articles of the treaty. The draft was presented to the General Assembly from September to December 1948 at the Palais de Chaillot in Paris. **Lemkin, with little money and suffering from recurring ill health, managed to make the Paris Conference and was present when the treaty was adopted on December 9, 1948. On December 11, the United States was the first of a required twenty Member State signatures needed for UN treaty adoption,** though it was also necessary for each individual signatory government to ratify and adopt the treaty as well. In this respect, one hurdle remained for United States ratification: approval by the U.S. Senate. On June 16, 1949, the treaty, supported by President Truman and the State Department, arrived in Congress where it immediately ran into roadblocks, including the Korean War, McCarthyism, rising xenophobia in the U.S., the disapproval of the American Bar Association, *and a movement to stop ratification led by Senator John Bricker.* Ultimately, the hurdles in the United States proved too high, and in April 1953, Secretary of State John Foster Dulles withdrew any human rights treaties from consideration. Lemkin was devastated by the actions of his adopted country.

After the UN adoption of the treaty in 1948, Lemkin became a minor celebrity, with newspaper articles written, magazine interviews given, and radio plays performed about his life. He enjoyed his brief time in the spotlight but continued to push for the ratification of the treaty in the United States. **He believed that with the U.S. in the moral lead, other countries would follow suit and provide positive** action in stopping mass race killings. He worked tirelessly during this period, becoming the first lecturer on international law at Yale University, consulting with the United Nations, working with the U.S. Committee for a U.N. Genocide Convention, writing his autobiography and drafting the unfinished manuscript, "HISTORY OF GENOCIDE". In addition to teaching at Yale, Lemkin taught at Rutgers and Princeton Universities. He was nominated for the Nobel Peace Prize in the early 1950's and received the Grand Cross of Cespedes from Cuba in 1950 and the Stephen Wise Award of the American Jewish Congress in 1951. Ill health continuously plagued him, in particular high blood pressure, which may have contributed to his death from a heart attack on August 28, 1959. He died in poverty, without marrying, and is buried in Mt. Hebron Cemetery in Queens, New York with a headstone that reads "The Father of the Genocide Convention."

The Convention on the Prevention and Punishment of the Crime of Genocide treaty went into effect by the United Nations on January 21, 1951. The United States ratified the treaty on October 14, 1988 and President Ronald Reagan signed the bill on November 4, 1988.

My second, great, dachshund………………DASSIE

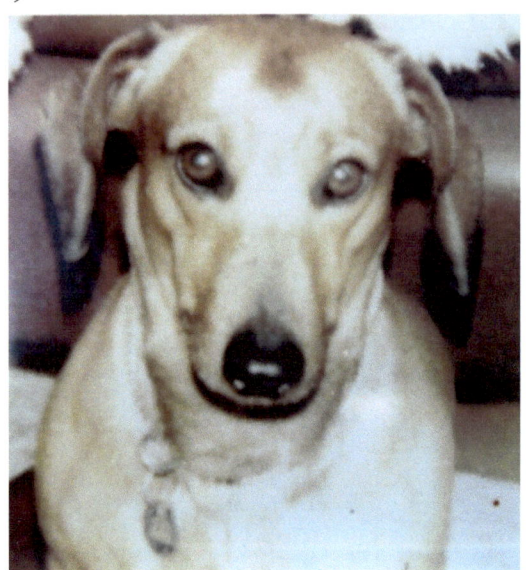

Many years later, my late niece, TRACEY, bought us a tan dachshund, for only $A20.00 again, that was bred from two miniatures, but he kept growing to a full size. I named him DASSIE, and he was given to us when I was 30 years old in 1973, and was sleeping on, and in my bed for 9 years until I left to be married and lived in California for our first year. It was so hard to leave him, which he knew as I comforted him for an hour before I left home.

Dassie slept on my bed at night on top of the blankets, starting at my feet, but when I awoke I would find him under the covers sleeping beside by body against my side, and with his nose pressed to my shoulder. My sister, Dawn took him over for the rest of his life and he lived firstly at Maroubra, by the ocean, and later, on the country-like Central Coast of New South Wales in great comfort. I saw him many times again after returning to Sydney a year later, in 1983, until he had to be put down with kidney failure at 15 years. I know he recognized me, but he was very happy with his other family. He was also God's gift in telling me He had forgiven me with the way I had treated my Karl.

Enter ROBBIE.

Then came Robbie, as a fully grown four-year-old in December, 1995. Third of three wonderful male, full-sized dachshunds.

(SON, STEVE'S HOME @ PLACERVILLE, CA)

Then came ROBBIE (The wonder dog)

When we arrived back in California from Australia in November, 1992, Robbie was already one year old and living with our son, Steve, and their 8 children in Placerville, California Gold country.

Robbie was named after his kennel name of "Robin Hood". He was the dog of their eldest son and our first grandson, Matthew. He usually barked at us incessantly. We saw him a few more times either when they came to Ben Lomond or at home when we visited, until our Pre-Christmas visit in December,1995, the day after Robbie had severely bitten their regular, daily U.P.S. driver, and Steve was going to have Robbie "put down". There was no reason why he bit the man, they said.

Phillip with ROBBIE & 2 of 3 Grandsons @ Placerville,Ca, MATTHEW and JOHN before he lived with us. Is that Elizabeth behind her big brother?

Matthew had not been able to look after Robbie very well because he was working and living in another town, and son, Steve was given another, larger beagle dog, with a cage that served as bed and housing <u>outside</u> the house, so they put little Robbie outside with the other dog

(Matthew has become the father of 2 sons & 2 daughters to his wonderful wife, Regan.)

But, when we saw that Robbie was no longer living inside the house besides Matthew's bed, and was sharing a stark, metal caged area with larger beagle in the front yard, we were surprised. There were a few sheets of newspaper on the sleeping area, and ONE feed bowl for BOTH dogs. Robbie was cold and starving, having to fight the other dog for his food. **Dachshunds are NEVER OUTSIDE DOGS, and this was WINTER**.

Had we come up to Placerville for that Pre-Christmas family sharing a couple of days earlier or later we probably would not

HAVE HAD TWELVE YEARS OF EXTREME JOY AND HAPPINESS WITH THAT DOG. **GOD IS SO GOOD IN GIVING US A DOG THAT WE NEVER ASKED HIM FOR. BUT HE KNEW MY HEART & PASSION FOR DACHSHUNDS.**

WE INSTANTLY SAID THAT WE WOULD TAKE HIM EVEN THOUGH WE HAD NO SPACE FOR ANY DOG WHERE WE LIVED. **ROBBIE HAD COME TO KNOW US BY THEN, AND WHEN WE OPENED THE SIDE DOOR OF THE VAN, HE IMMEDIATELY JUMPED INSIDE,** WITH HIS CARRY CASE, THAT WAS PREVIOUSLY HIS BED, HIS LEASH & COLLAR AND SOME FEED.

I BELIEVE THAT HAD WE ARRIVED BEFORE OR AFTER THAT DAY, WE WOULD NEVER HAVE SEEN ROBBIE COME HOME WITH US, **BECAUSE GOD'S TIMING IS ALWAYS PERFECT. NEVER ON OUR TIMING, BUT NEVER LATE EITHER.**

When we arrived home, he slept inside his carry case that was also beside my side of the bed, but soon after we saw it was too small, so we placed a padded, wide chair into our confined room, and he loved it as **his new bed.** We also put another pillow under him and a blanket over him, since that was the way my previous dachshund slept in Australia from 1973 -1982 when I left for America. As I said, Dassie lived with my sister after I left for America for the first trip and lived until 1988, when he was 15 yrs. He was also a full-sized dog from miniature parents. Just kept on growing.

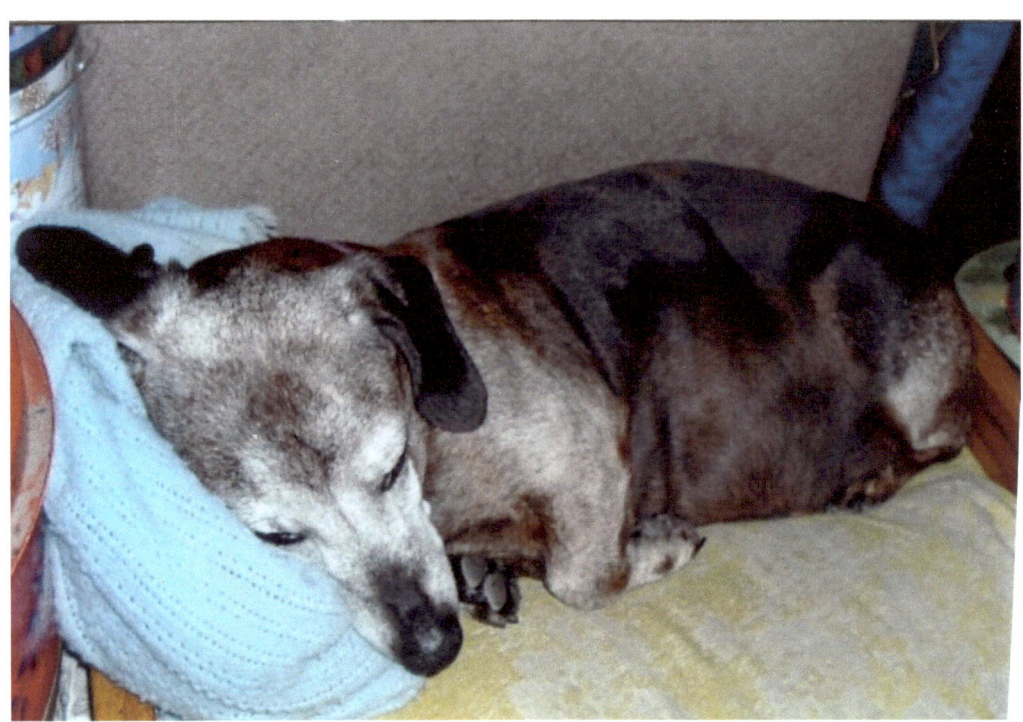

Robbie did not like anything being placed on his bed, and would get down if we put something beside him, and if there was something there when he was on the floor, Robbie would look up at the bed and bark loudly just once.

In the latter years we had to cut 6" from the chair legs to help Robbie not hurt his shoulder when he jumped down. He was able to jump up and down easily, even at the end. But before cutting the chair legs lower, several times he could not jump down without hurting his shoulders as he jumped either onto the concrete floor where we live under Linda's mother, Holly's house, or the bitumen roadway from the car seat so we solved that by cutting the legs of his bed/chair and helping him from the car in need.

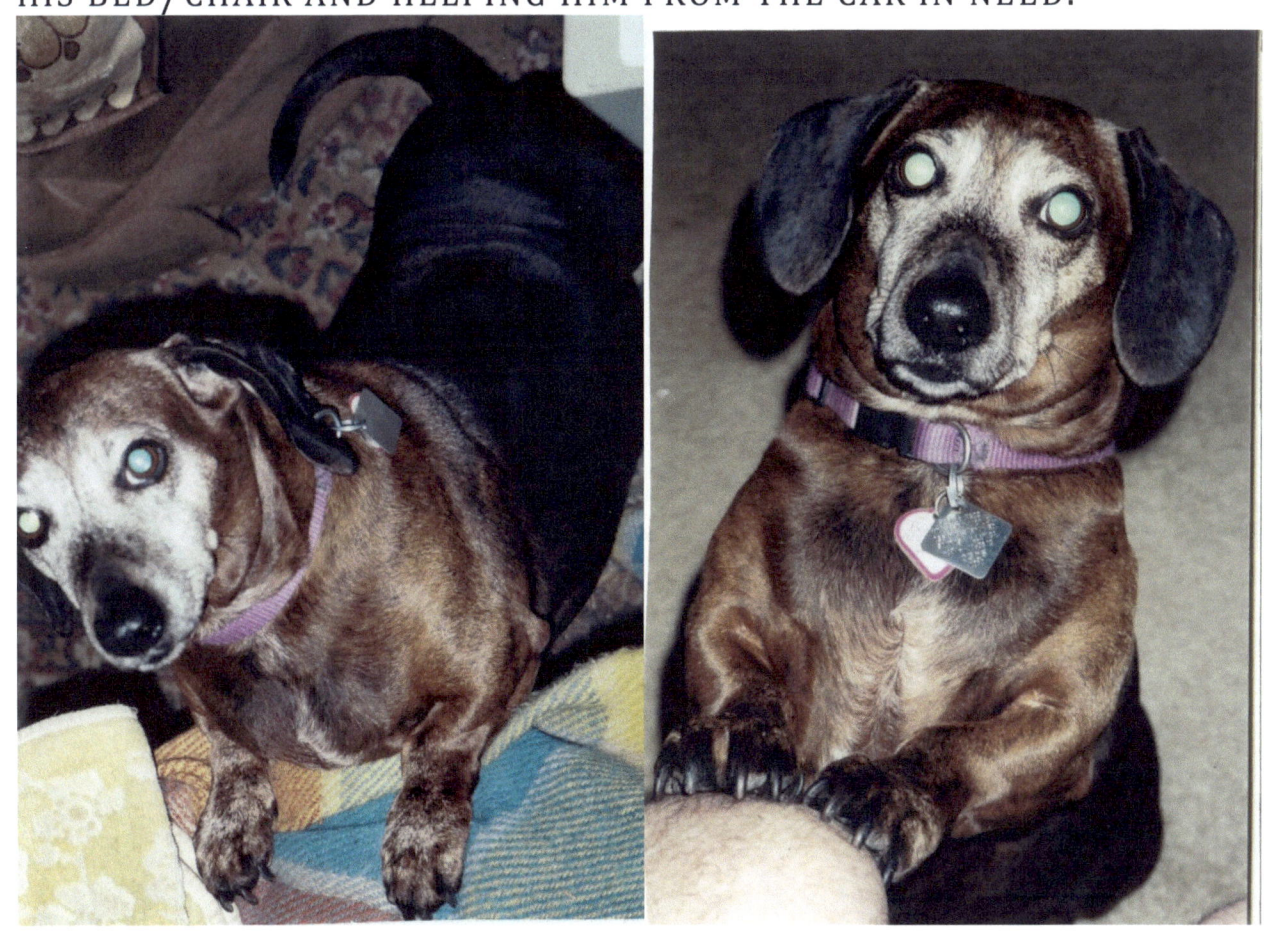

What a memory Robbie had

ONCE, AND ONLY ONCE WAS ENOUGH FOR ROBBIE TO REMEMBER SOMETHING. ONE DAY I SAID TO LINDA, "COME ON" AND ROBBIE IMMEDIATELY JUMPED ONTO OUR SOFA CHAIR AND STRAIGHT ONTO OUR HIGH MATTRESS, BED. I SAID, "NOT YOU, ROBBIE", AND PICKED HIM UP TO PUT HIM BACK ONTO HIS OWN BED. **THE ONLY OTHER TIME WE EVER HAD ROBBIE ON OUR BED WAS THE LAST WEDNESDAY BEFORE I TOOK HIM TO THE VETERINARY, WHEN HE HAD HIM SLEEP BETWEEN US.**

THIS DOUBLE BED WAS BUILT IN 1836 AND CAME FROM THE HOME OF THE FIRST SENATOR FROM IOWA. IT CAME WITH A MATCHING DRESSER WITH A LARGE MIRROR. THE BEDHEAD IS 7'3" HIGH. IT IS A FAMILY INHERITANCE.

A Very Obese Dog

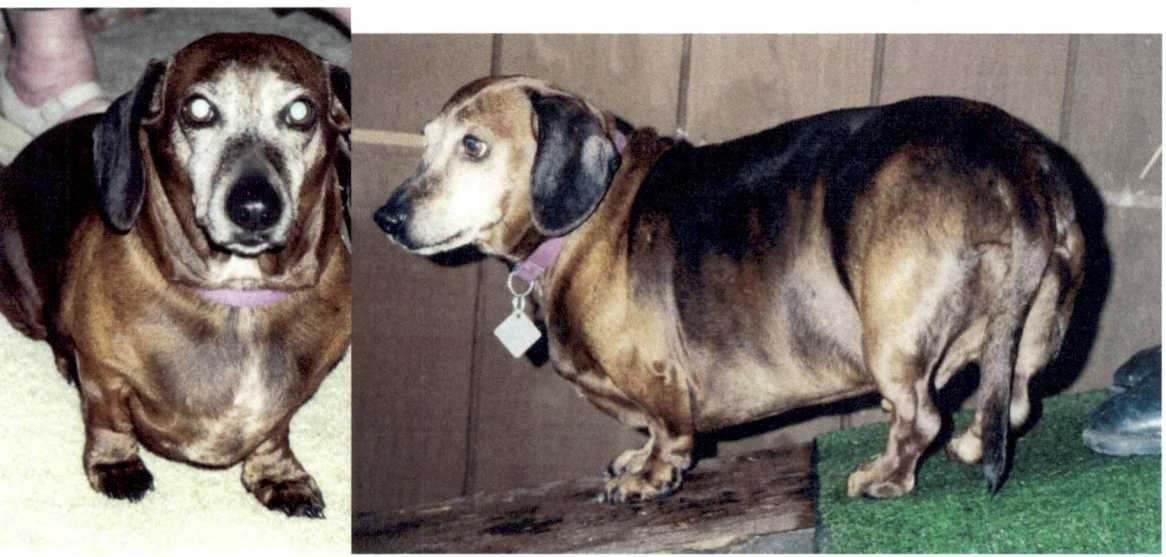

WALKING THE PLANK

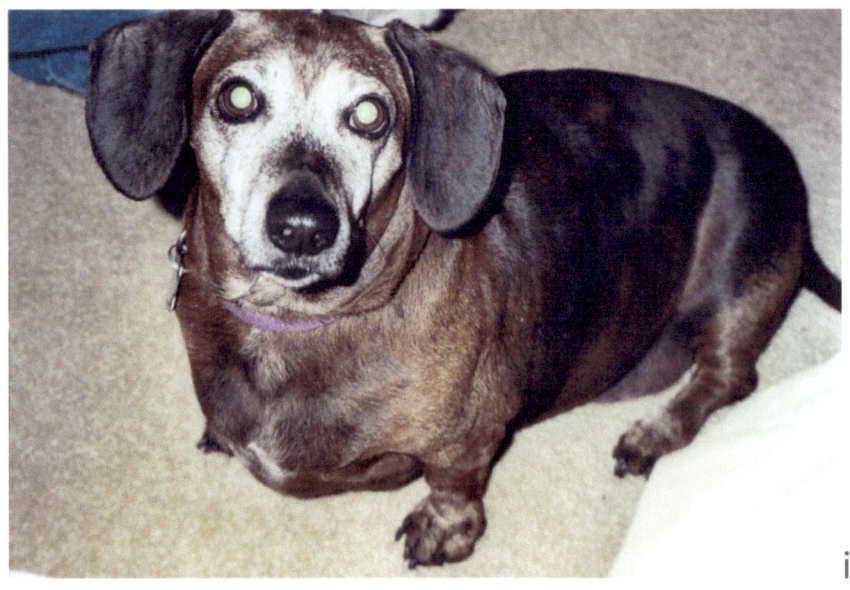

it's those ears

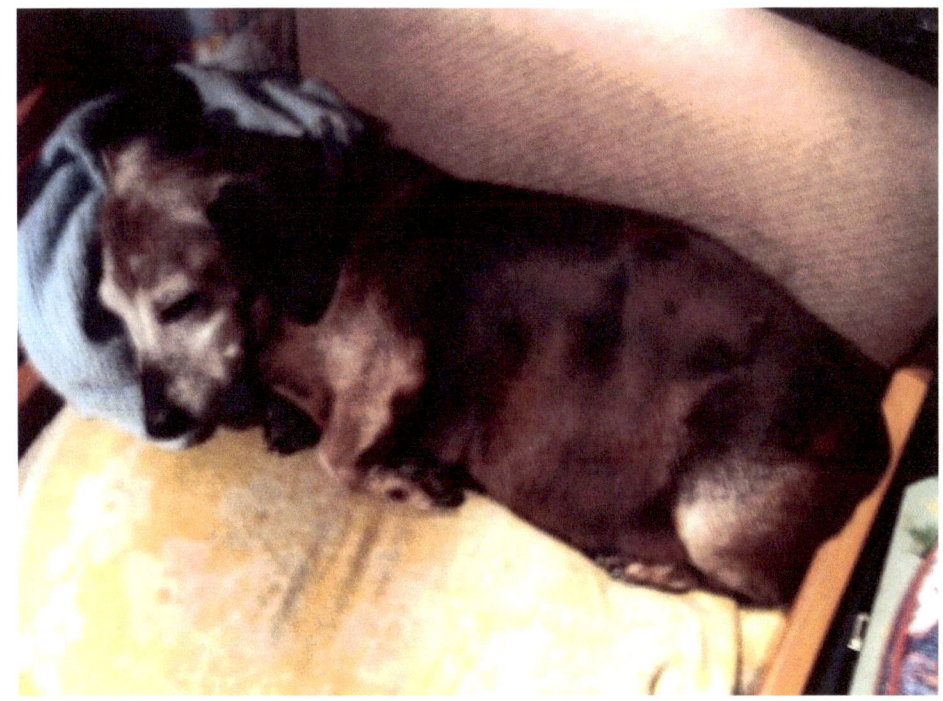

About five years before, we changed his feed to **Flint River Ranch Dog Food** and he put on a lot of weight because of the **higher nutrition. He weighed 35.4 lbs and was obese.** The vet told us to cut his food intake in **half** and exercise Robbie **daily**, so we walked daily around Mt Hermon when I went for our mail. Over the next 2 summers he took off all of the excess weight. **We took off ten pounds** and he weighed **25 lbs** over the last year of his life.

We were told that his father was a miniature Dachshund and his mother a full-sized one, but with a Labrador cross in his heritage somewhere. Robbie was a full-size but with stronger than normal back and shoulders, and he never had the slightest problem with his legs or back other than the few times when he hurt himself jumping down over the last year of his life as he started to show his age.

Once, several years ago Robbie jumped over the back seat & out of the rear window of our Ford Aerostar Van onto the roadway without hurting himself. It was a long way down for him. We made sure that the rear window was wound up after that effort.

He was a **very healthy dog**, because we never allowed him to eat anything except his feed, fruit and vegetables that he loved. Except for occasional scrounging he never ate any junk food or anything of poor nutrition. We had a small garbage content because Robbie was there to eat the ends, skins, peels, banana, pear, apple cores, etc, as well as share celery, lettuce ends, tomatoes, sweet potatoes, cucumbers, and especially **radishes and carrots & apples**. It was funny to watch him jump up and catch the peels. When he first came home with us he could not catch a thing, and the food would just bounce off from his nose as he tried to catch it, but I taught him how to catch.

Floating on air?

The Hunter Dog

Robbie had very good senses all his life and never lost his trailing ability. It was funny to hide and watch Robbie chasing my trail looking for me, with his nose to the ground while scooting past me sitting on a swing seat, or behind a covering, and coming back to find me. He was very good at trailing. His senses were good to the end. Never any loss of hearing, smell or sight despite his age.

Ball games he avoided after I accidentally hit him with a tennis ball ONCE. That was all it took. NO MORE BALL GAMES, EVER AGAIN. Balloons he did NOT like. What do you think I am, A DOG? Nor did he ever chase anything thrown. Just to look up as if to say, "You threw it, get it yourself"

A HUNTER and a DIGGER with extreme bravery, Robbie would dig down through the hard clay very fast and have his head buried in the dirt within 2 minutes chasing an animal below ground. Raccoons he treated the same. We have a few around here all the time. Once he caught a gopher in about 4 seconds in the ivy outside our door.

That last July, he came inside with a severe wound on his rear, and we could only assume it was a daylight attack after Robbie has cornered another Raccoon and was bitten from behind.

(Warning: graphic photos)

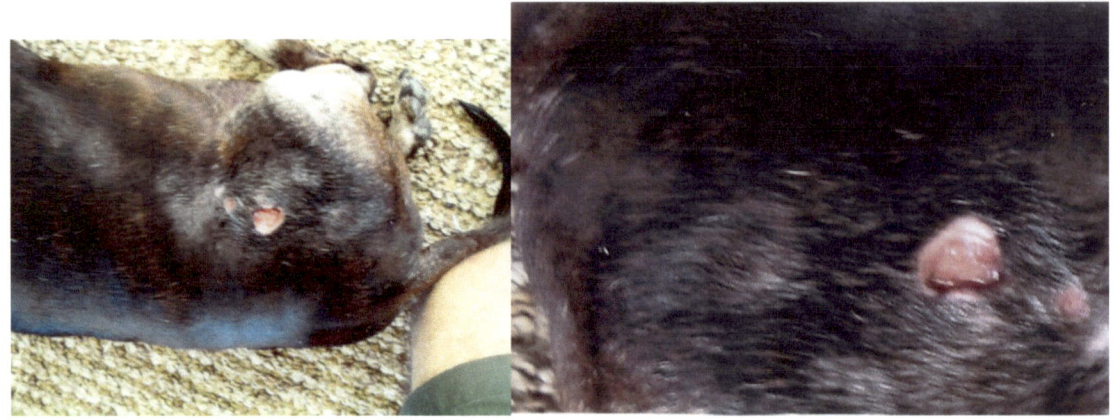

8TH JULY, 2007   BITTEN & VERY SORE

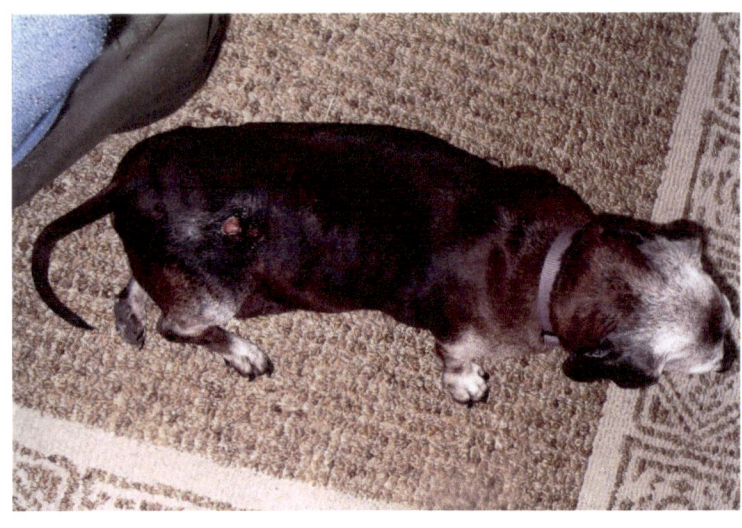

I HAD SEEN HIM CHASE THEM AWAY BEFORE. HE NEVER BOTHERED THE SQUIRRELS THAT FEED AROUND THE HOUSE ALL THE TIME. AFTER A VISIT TO THE VET, PAIN SHOTS AND ANTI-BIOTICS, WITH SPECIAL TREATMENT WITH **SHARK LIVER OIL & L-ARGININE TO PROMOTE FAST WOUND HEALING**, ROBBIE WAS BACK ON HIS FEET, CHASING A RACCOON AT 4:00 AM **JUST 4 DAYS LATER**, <u>AFTER</u> INTENSE PRAYER **OVER THE PHONE THE NIGHT BEFORE.**

I HAD COME ACROSS THE USE OF L-ARGININE FROM THE WATSONVILLE HOSPITAL WOUND CENTER THAT THEY SUGGEST FOR HEALING OPEN ULCERS AND BED SORES. FOR THE THREE DAYS AFTER BEING ATTACKED HE WAS IN PAIN AND JUST LAY STILL ON HIS BED. WE HAD TO HELP HIM GET DOWN AND UP TO GO TO THE BATHROOM AND TO EAT.

HE WAS TOTALLY HEALED IN 2 WEEKS.

BUT THE VET WARNED OF THE UNDERLINE FIRST SIGN OF A HEART MURMUR BACK IN JULY, 2007. HE WAS, THOUGH, GREATLY IMPRESSED BY THE RAPID, CLEAN HEALING PROCESS IN ROBBIE'S DEEP WOUND. I READ LATER THAT THE SAME L-ARGININE IS GOOD FOR THE CARDIO-VASCULAR SYSTEM.

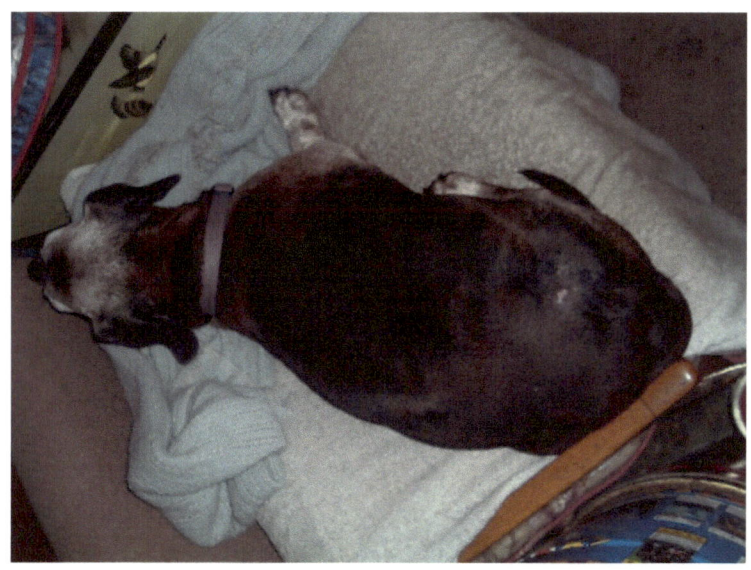

23RD JULY, 2007   HEALED ALREADY

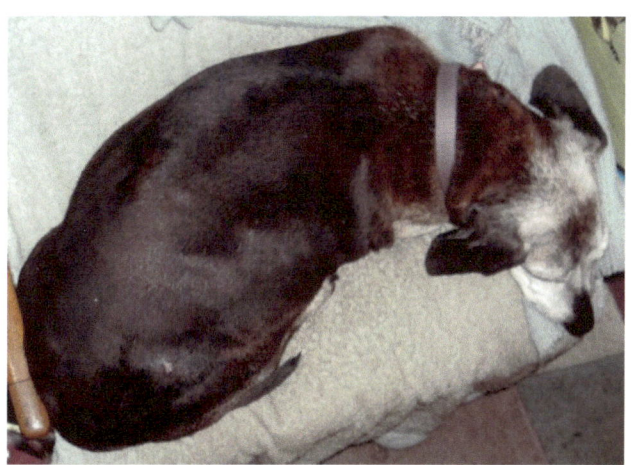

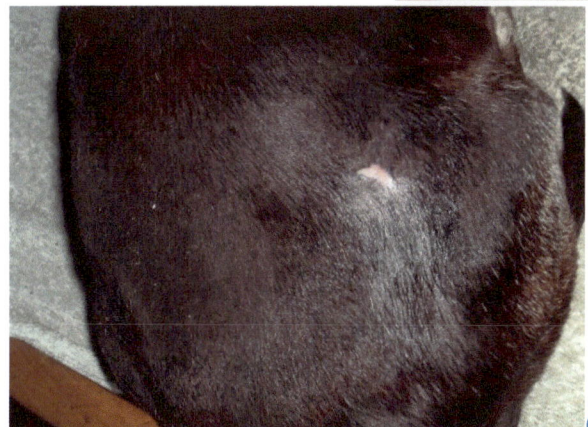

CLOSE-UP - NO SCAR!

TOTALLY HEALED

Another attack on Robbie

One night he came inside looking very strange & I thought it was a BEE STING, as we have the yellow jackets nesting around us every year despite my destroying their nests. It was quite an ALLERGY response. HIS FACE SWELLED UP TWICE ITS SIZE. Benadryl & Prednisone took quick, expensive emergency vet care of that. He looked so funny with a puffed up face, but I was very concerned over his bloated head and rushed him to the late night, 24 hr vet. Should have taken his photo but I very much concentrated upon his healing at the time.

He was normal again the next morning.

THEN THERE WAS THE BIG ATTACK

ANGELS CAMP, CA. VETS
- MIRACLE OF ANSWERED PRAYER.

OUR BIGGEST SCARE WAS WHEN HE WAS EIGHT, WE COULD HAVE LOST HIM IN NOVEMBER, 1999. ~ ~ ~

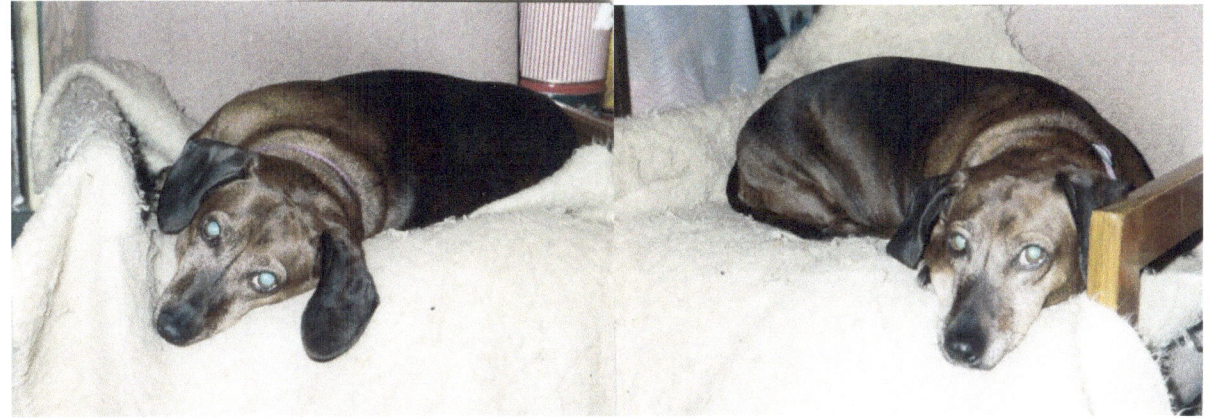

Photos of ROBBIE when very ill, BEFORE going to Angels Camp, CA

3 DAYS WITHOUT ANY FOOD, AFTER DIARRHEA AND THEN THROWING UP ON WATER, TAKING ROBBIE WITH US TO OUR FAMILY AT PLACERVILLE OVERNIGHT BEFORE WE LEFT FOR A RESORT WHERE NO PETS ALLOWED. OUR SON'S VETERINARIAN REFUSED TO LOOK AT HIM, SO WE TOOK HIM WITH US ON THE FLOOR OF FRONT SEAT OF OUR CAR. **WE REALLY KNEW THAT GOD HAD TO DO SOMETHING FAST OR WE WOULD LOSE HIM**.

WE DROVE PAST A LARGE VET. HOSPITAL- 2 STORIED BUILDING ON HIGHWAY 49# AT ANGELS' CAMP, CA.

We were going to check into resort first and then return Robbie to that vet, but when Robbie could not even hold water down we spun around to check him in, just 30 minutes before they closed that Friday night. They took one quick look and immediately put Robbie onto an I.V. drip, took X-Rays and put Bariameal beads into him to check X-Rays every hour for the next 48 hours.

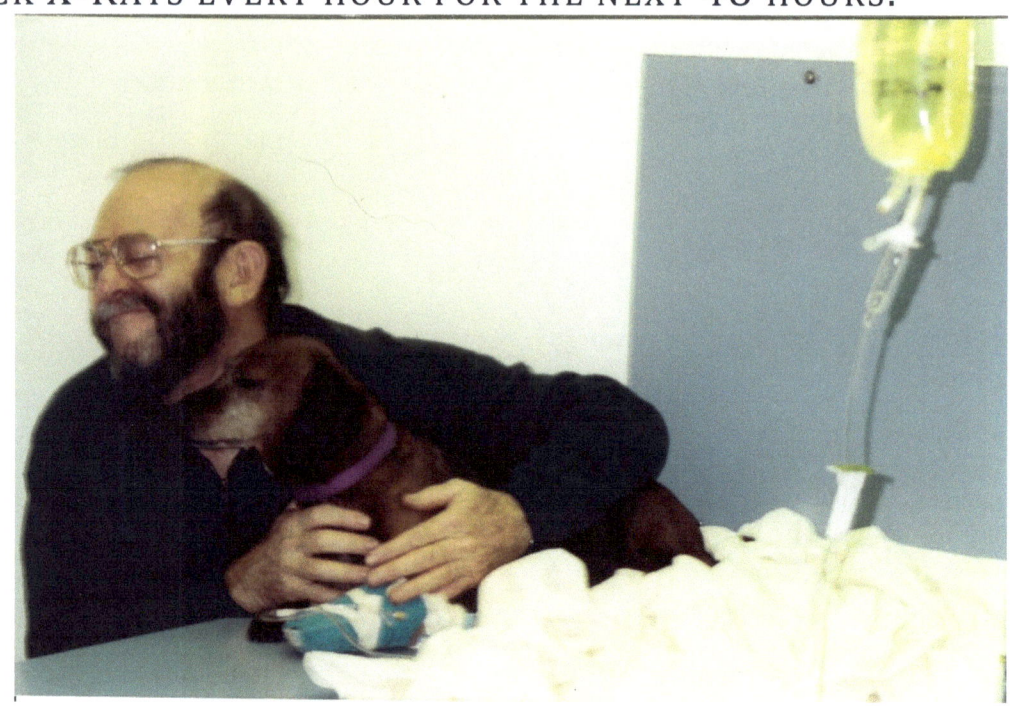

Robbie on the I/V drip before the operation, still lickin' good.

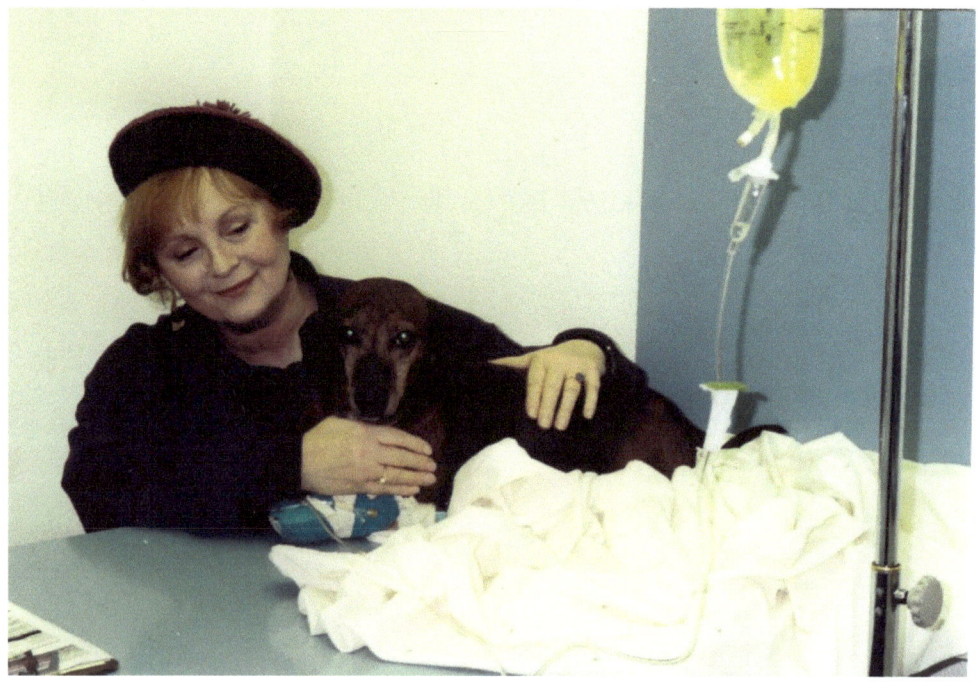

Linda with our Robbie

It was a <u>complete blockage with nothing passing through him.</u> Lots of gas bloated him, and must have caused him a lot of pain. We have one of those X-Rays. They even let us visit when they were closed for Sunday, and we took these photos of an excited Robbie with the I/V drip. on his front leg, expecting to go home. Alas, we had to leave and return late Monday, when the 2 owners told us they had to do a scope and then open him up if nothing was located, and they actually told us they thought it probably was cancer, afterwards.

We were requested to call them in the midst of the operation an hour later, when they told us that the moment they operated, he released all the gas pent up inside for so long and they found <u>NOTHING</u>. **They checked all his organs and said he was a very healthy dog in great condition. That was at 6 pm.**

<u>At 4 pm, we had laid hands on Robbie, anointed him with anointing oil from Israel, and prayed in Jesus' Name for God to dissolve all blockages.</u> They had absolutely NO EXPLANATION. We did not have any doubt that we should take him with us, yet, not having the faintest idea where some Vet would treat him. We did have a peace in our hearts.

We had to take out a Doggie Credit Card (with No interest over 12 months) and his photo on it to help pay them. *I said, if you found nothing then there was no cost, right? Wrong!* So Robbie had his own credit card (and Credit Score?) that we could use any time the bill was OVER $1,000. We called in the next morning on our way home, and they released him as he had completely recovered from the operation better than expected. We were so pleased with their total consideration and they even phoned us back home to check on Robbie a few days later.

With a six inch scar on his stomach to prove he was a miracle dog that lived for almost another 8 years after that close encounter with death. The funny thing was that about one week <u>after</u> that trauma, and <u>not</u> during it, <u>Robbie suddenly turned very grey over his head and face.</u> He proceeded to get almost white over the last year.

HE STARTED OUT AS A BRINDLE DOG, UNLIKE ANY REGULAR DACHSHUND COLOR WE HAD SEEN BEFORE, AND THEN OVER THE YEARS, LOST HAIRS FROM HIS BACK, RE-GREW MOST OF THEM IN A DARKER SHADE OF RED, YET HAD THIS GREY MASK OVER HIS EYES AND SNOUT.

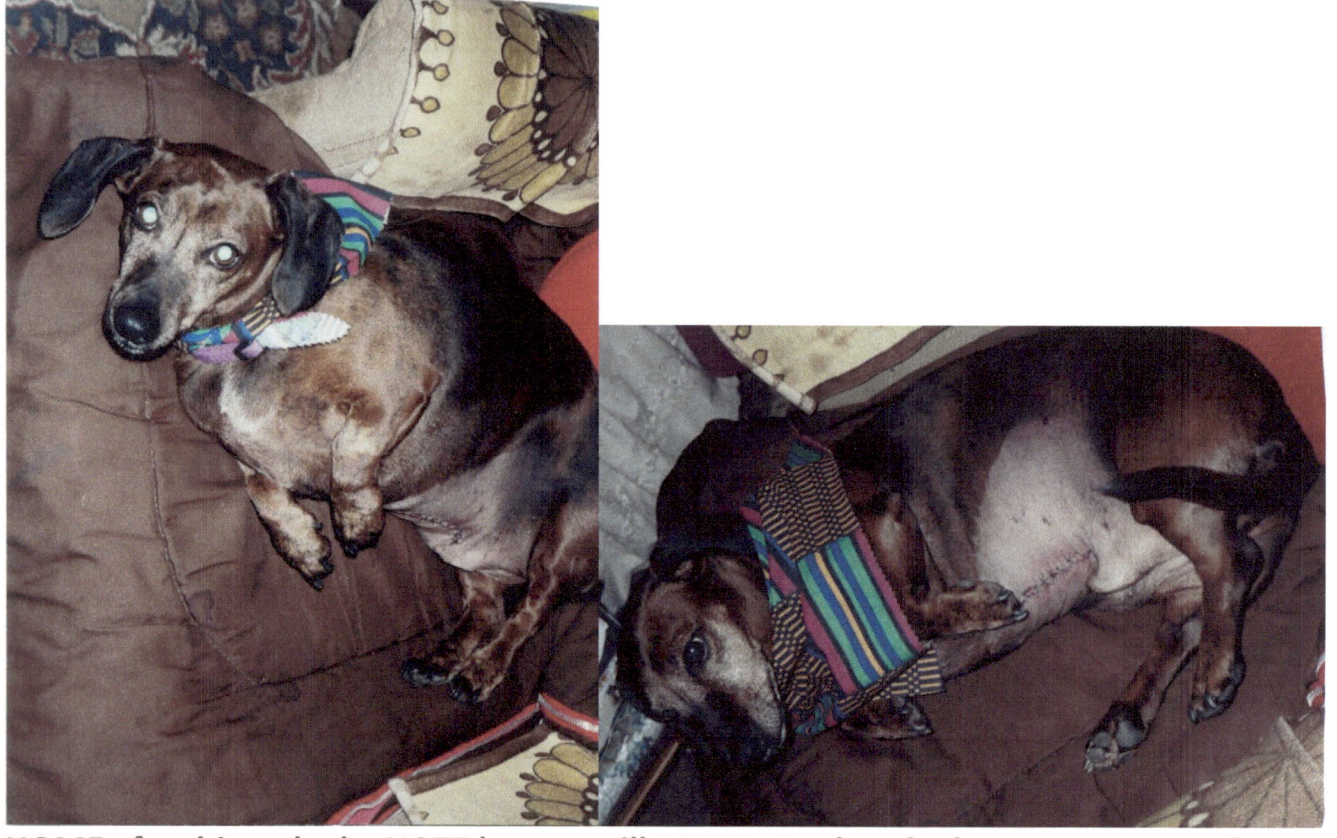

HOME after his ordeal ~ NOTE he was still BRINDLE colored. The vets put a scarf around his neck.

WE HAD THE STITCHES REMOVED A WEEK LATER BY OUR LOCAL VET, WHO WAS NOT VERY NICE TO US. IF WE HAD LEFT ROBBIE WITH THEM WE WOULD HAVE REGRETTED IT, AND IT IS MOST UNLIKELY THAT WE WOULD HAVE HAD ANY PEACE ON OUR VACATION & WE NEVER WENT BACK TO THAT ONE AND FOUND ANOTHER VET. WHO IS FABULOUS.

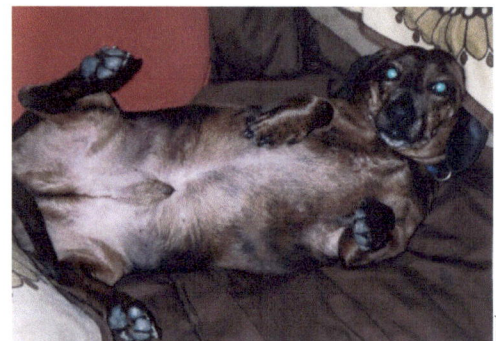

look at that scar!

ROBBIE was always FAMILY, going with us everywhere

MONTEVALLE WASH UP:

WE ALWAYS TOOK HIM WITH US WHEREVER WE DROVE, AND ONE REGULAR SPOT WAS THE MILL DINING HALL OF A MOBILE HOME PARK THAT WE WASHED AND CLEANED UP AT AFTER DINNER EVENTS. ONE NIGHT WE LOCKED UP AT MIDNIGHT, WHEN WE THOUGHT HE WENT OUT TO OUR CAR., ONLY TO SEE HIM STILL WALKING AROUND INSIDE, LOOKING AT US THROUGH A CLOSED DOOR. WE HAD TO WAKE UP A NEIGHBOR WITH THE DOOR KEY TO GET HIM OUT AND GO HOME.

ROBBIE ATE THE SALAD AND MEAT LEFTOVERS IN THE KITCHEN FOR SEVERAL YEARS, UNTIL THEY BARRED HIM. HE WAS CLEANER THAN MOST PEOPLE. IS THAT WHY HE PUT ON WEIGHT? HE WOULD GET SO EXCITED AS WE DROVE INSIDE THE STREET HEADING TOWARDS THE PARK.

WE HAD TO LEAVE HIM AT HOME THEREAFTER.

WORK WITH ME-

Lots of places where I did yard work or outside jobs is where I usually took him with me. He always recognized a house or area that we had come to before long before we arrived at the spot.

Once, when I was at a friend's home splitting wood blocks for him as a day's work, Robbie was sniffing around his back yard and checking out the cul-de-sac street outside, when we suddenly lost him and called and called to no avail. Robbie always stayed close to me whenever I did any yard work, etc. That day, we just could not find him for a few minutes, when the next door neighbor came out of his corner house, asking if the dog inside his kitchen, looking up at the refrigerator belonged to me.

I said "Come on Robbie, you won't get any carrots there, come back here where you belong," and apologized to the bewildered neighbor, who had left his front door slightly ajar. Robbie had a very strong snout and could push open the heaviest of doors. Even a sliding glass door that was just opened a quarter of an inch was all he needed to get inside when he wanted to. In any house for the first time he would sniff around the whole house until he covered every room, even if they had no animals. It was just his habit to be inquisitive.

Usually every week we worked on the gardens, trees and yard at Dr Stan's home. He walked with me every time I moved around, but then decided it was easier to lie on top of the retaining wall looking down at me, as I worked below him. Occasionally he would go chasing a deer, and once he wandered next door up the hill to a neighbor's back yard, eating their gardener's Danish pastry that he left on a plate that was on the ground as he worked up the hill.

A cry came out, **"Hey, your dog ate my Danish,"** to which I replied, **"He likes coffee with his Danish."**

Robbie is so gentle when he sneaks someone's food left lying on a plate on the ground. He takes it up and retires to a quiet spot to sample the stolen delicacy. I arrived to see him finish off the Danish as the gardener yelled out, about 20 yards away around the corner of a shed.

Robbie liked to anticipate our leaving work and would run back towards our car several times when I started to walk in a direction that included pushing a wheelbarrow or carrying garden refuse. It didn't matter that I was not actually headed for the car, Robbie would run to that direction anyway. He would look back and turn around, running towards me then run again to the car. When I told him it was time to go home he would run and jump into the front passenger seat as soon as I could open the door.

When he was tired of walking down the hill with me he would just walk on top of a seven feet high retaining wall and lie down with his face towards me watching while I worked. He always had the same patterns of jumping off the end where the height of the wall drew close to a pathway.

He would also walk along the top of the wall above the swimming pool, that was only about 8" wide and 7 feet tall, rather than the small path beside the top of the wall where the garden was. He had no fears, although he could make me feel slightly anxious. He always wanted to be close to me as I worked. If I shut the gate with him outside the pool area, once he went up the top and found a way to get under the fence, by digging through and then coming to sit beside me.

WHO? ME?

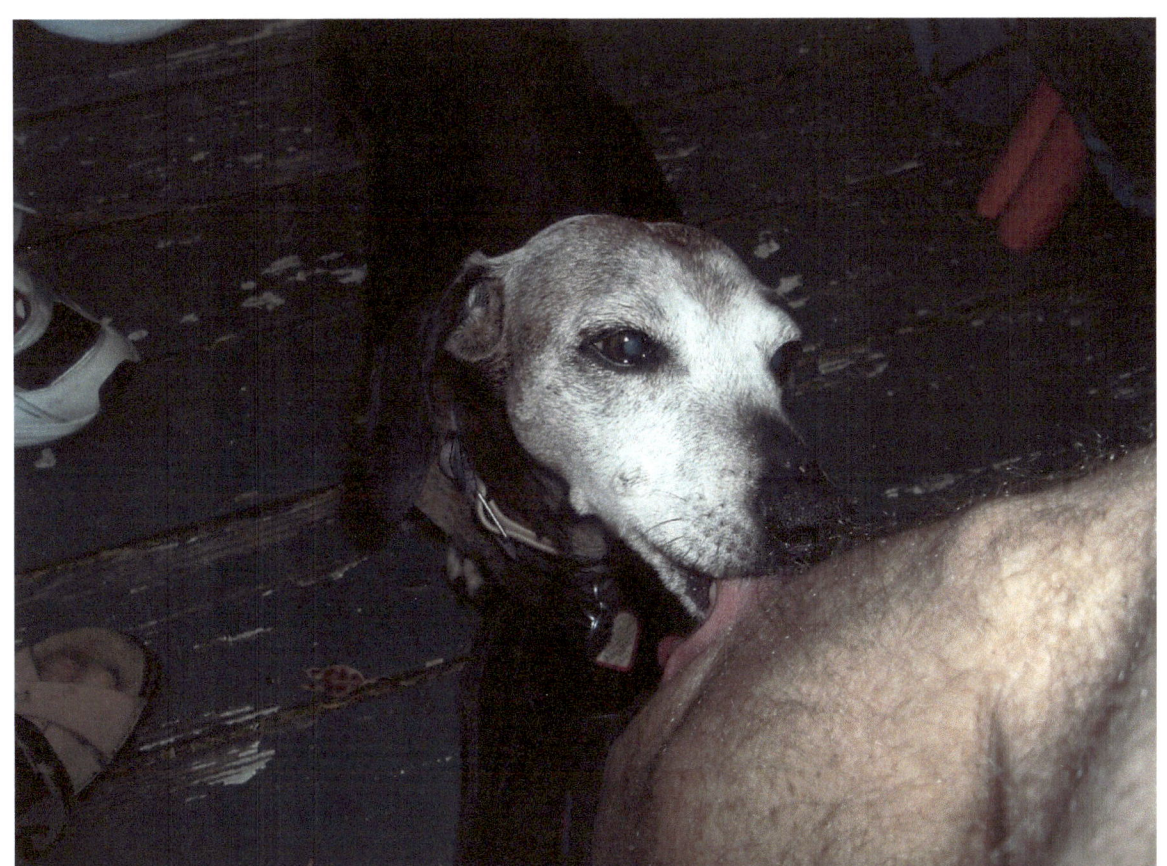

Never mind that "finger-lickin' good CHICKEN, THIS LEG IS O.K."

Once at a Bar-B-Que with students at Bethany College, I watched as he gently extruded a piece of chicken off a girl's plate, leaving the salad. It was too late to stop him. They had left two plates unattended to go back for their drinks. This was Robbie's opportunity for a snack. He dropped the chicken onto the grass, looked appreciatively at his catch, and was about to eat it when I yelled at him. He turned and left it on the grass. They did not want it back, so I ate it. The grass was clean. Chicken bones can be harmful to dogs. But I did give him other meat bones regularly, sometimes raw.

OUT IN THE BUSH ONE DAY WHEN HE WAS YOUNG AND FAST. —

(REMEMBER THOSE DACHSHUND RACES ON TV?) - I LEFT HIM BEHIND BECAUSE HE WOULD NOT COME TO THE CAR AFTER A LONG DAY'S WORK- SO, I MADE ROBBIE RUN AFTER THE CAR ALONG A LONG, CARLESS, DIRT TRACK FOR ABOUT ½ MILE, UNTIL HE STOPPED AND STOOD THERE LOOKING AT THE CAR GOING AWAY, UNTIL I CAME BACK AND LOVED HIM. HE DID NOT KNOW WHY I DID THAT, AND WOULD NOT DO IT AGAIN. BUT I WAS TIRED AND WANTED TO GO HOME AND HE JUST WOULD NOT COME TO THE CAR.

I REMEMBERED WHEN I WAS ABOUT 10 YEARS OLD WITH KARL, THAT WE VISITED SOME FRIENDS AND FORGOT ABOUT OUR DOG AS WE STARTED TO DRIVE HOME WITHOUT HIM. I SUDDENLY REALIZED HE WAS NOT IN OUR CAR AND LOOKED OUT THE REAR WINDOW TO SEE HIM RUNNING ALONG THE ROAD BEHIND US AS WE DROVE DOWN THE END OF THEIR STREET. I YELLED AT MY MUM TO STOP THE CAR, "HEY, WE FORGOT ABOUT KARL."

NO, THIS IS NOT ROBBIE

BUT, WE COULD NOT RESIST THIS METAL BOBBLE-HEAD DACHSHUND FROM KLAMATH FALLS, OREGON.

NO, NOT ROBBIE, BUT HE WAS ALSO A PATRIOT

My other pet~ a CAT!

We brought a Ginger cat, DANNY, from Australia when we arrived here in 1992. He lived upstairs with Linda's mother, Holly as we sent him here ahead of us about 6-8 weeks before we arrived and he suddenly became an indoor cat because of the torrential daily rains that year in 1992. He was also a great hunter, often bringing in a prize catch.

In Australia, our daughter, Christina was visiting a friend up in the Blue Mountains (50 miles West of Sydney), after their cat gave them a litter of ginger kittens. My wife called me at home and they cornered me to bring one home with them, in a box (see photo) on the train. Dad, he is so pretty and so quiet, and will keep the varmits away, and he is an outdoor cat.

There were only two encounters when Robbie Chased Danny, when Danny turned and scratched Robbie's NOSE TWICE, and then they were distant friends after that. Danny died in 1998 from Cancer that the rotten pet food here gave him, when he was only 12 yrs. They both had a very docile nature. Strange, but we just noticed that BOTH DANNY & ROBBIE were born on 1st November, in different years.

Danny loved to lie inside cardboard boxes left opened.

This is his first photo the day he came to live with us at Oatley.

Or lie behind us.

Robbie liked to lie in the sun on the front deck

Robbie was very sensitive to the Spirit realm

Bailing up and snarling at 2 young grand-daughters in a friend's home, where her daughter was staying temporarily at the time, caused a stir. "What's wrong with your dog?" our friend asked.

I replied, "NOTHING, but what is wrong with the evil spirits in your house?" Robbie sensed the evil and would NOT allow them to pass. I had to pull him back. He would not stop snarling at them. He never did that again, before or afterwards

Another time was more interesting for us. At home Linda decided to move the painting her mother had painted in 1980 of the Children in the Fire- "Little Embers" from the office wall and place it above the back of our bed on the wall above our heads. Robbie was lying on his raised chair-bed opposite the wall, and when we placed the painting into his view, he sat up and <u>stared at the painting transfixed for about 20 minutes before he again laid down</u>. He never looked at this painting again after it stayed on the wall.

When we had a man of God invite us down to his home at Grover Beach, CA (Pismo) for 3 days, he said it was O.K. to bring Robbie with us. **Robbie would NOT leave his anointing the whole time we were with Jerry. When Jerry was on his face before the Lord in his bedroom, Robbie would open his door and go and lick his face, when he sat in his lounge chair, Robbie would always lie under his feet, whenever he went into the kitchen, Robbie would go with him, looking up at him, and not just looking for food.**

Robbie would **ALWAYS** come into the center of people **PRAYING**, for otherwise he just laid himself on carpet and slept nearby. He was a PEOPLE DOG, and usually ignored other dogs when we walked, for he just loved human company. We always had him with us except wherever we could not have him inside or there was no Summer shade, or it was too cold, so Robbie was a 24 x 7 family dog. When we packed for any trip, he would lie on his bed watching us and waiting until the last minute to get down as we were about to leave, in case he did not have to "STAY UPSTAIRS WITH Grandma." To watch his disappointment in his eyes and his ears drop was sad, and he looked for our return at the front door each day we were away. When we called, he always recognized our voice over the phone. He was happy to just come with us and sleep in the car, even for hours.

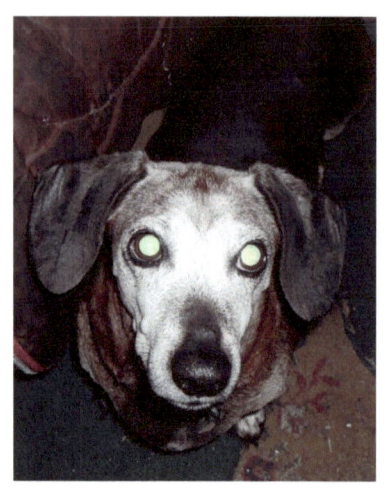

PRAYER WALKING IN CHINATOWN, OAKLAND

Robbie was able to get us into every building with LOCKED GATES.

Someone was coming out as we walked up to each and every one and they all opened the gates for us to go inside because of our little dog. We were walking along the hot streets in 104 degree heat, and they all wanted to get water for our dog.

We knew we would not have been able to enter ANY of those buildings and locked apartments without Robbie. We knew no-one in that part of Oakland, yet we were able to have Robbie get every locked gate opened by someone as we went from house to house. Language was no barrier as everyone spoke to our dog with great kindness. We were able to pray with several of these people that day, thanks to the Lord through Robbie.

Robbie went to more prayer meetings and churches than most people attend. (We never gave him a Bark Mitzvah) **He could bark in tongues, but rarely would interpret.** BUT, Robbie could read your mind and know exactly what you were about to do. When we could not take him with us on trips he reluctantly went upstairs to stay with Holly, sleeping in a large rocker armchair, but he kept looking for us to return at night. As I shared, he responded to our voices over the phone.

Help me up

Robbie softly barked just once whenever he wanted to get up into his bed after going outside at night, opening the most heavy doors, but of course he would not close them after coming back inside. He could always hear the animals outside even when asleep, then jumping down pushing the door open and barking, waking us up. Then we would have to get up, lift him up and close the door.

Sometimes, he would scratch first on a closed door and then bark once. Usually in someone else's home he would just LOOK at the door, front or back, or even ANY door, telling us quietly that he wanted to go outside. **Once we were sitting there watching the TV, and Robbie started to bark and scratch at the mirror on the armoire beside the TV, so we opened the armoire door 2 or 3 times and he just looked at us, and we discovered he just wanted us to get up and open the door for him to go outside. He could have just pushed it open himself. He was a very intelligent dog.**

ROBBIE SLOWING DOWN AS HE CAME TO THE END OF HIS LIFE.

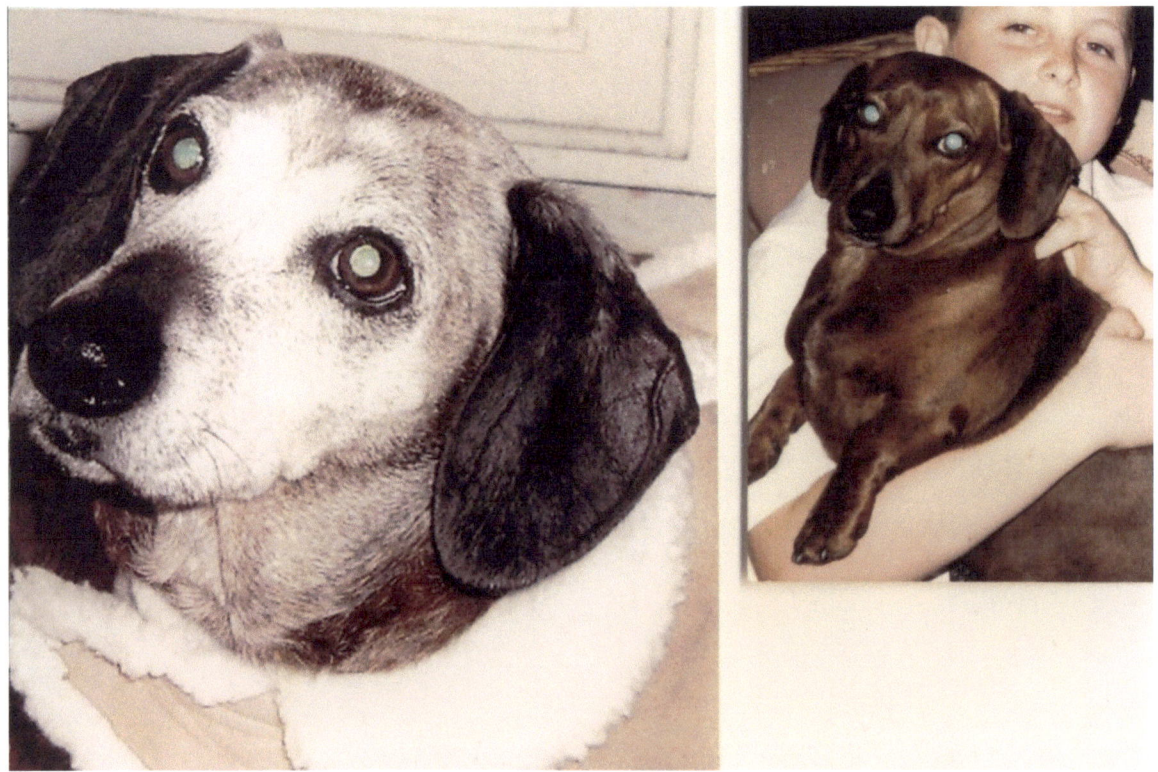

COMPARE THESE TWO PHOTOS OF ROBBIE TAKEN ABOUT 10 YEARS APART.

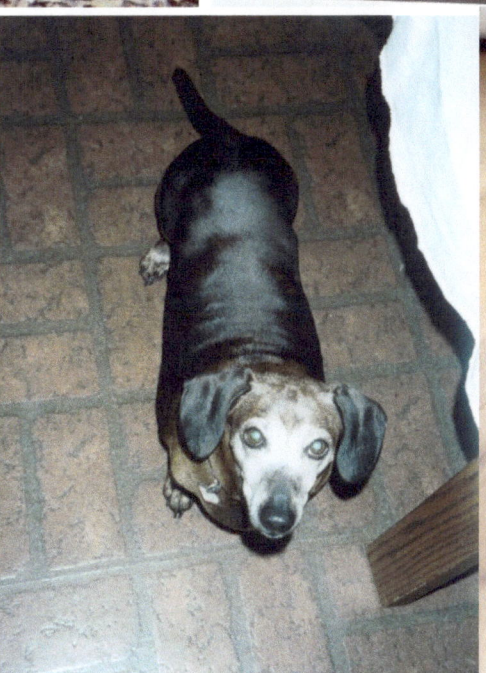

After a few rousings earlier in his life, Robbie NEVER ever walked across any road and would stay on the street only IF we were walking together, so we could trust him to stay away from traffic, if we let him go outside. He had a good respect for cars, but would walk up to someone driving into where we were, just close enough for them not to see him, but far enough away not to approach the moving vehicle. His intelligence was really amazing. Whenever I went out to the street, Robbie would come out to look for me, walking slowly to either the right or left up to the next dwelling, but always on the left side of our road up to the cul-de-sac that ends about 6 houses up the hill. He kept off the other side of the street except when we walked together. Even if we walked a long way around the local streets, he would always run ahead of me and look around to see if I was still coming. When I said "Robbie come home" he would turn and run past me, always trying to get home first.

When I would call out to him, "Robbie, COME EAR, or COME 'ERE", he would drop his ears down and wait for me to come and stroke his ears, and if I called, "Come HERE", he would always come to me. He KNEW the difference!

REMEMBERING THE DIFFERENCES IN MY DOGS

With my other dog, Dassie, we lived across the road from a Westfield Shopping Center that was built after we moved into the Home Unit (Condominium to you) on the 3rd floor of 4 floors. The ground floor was a parking area and garages. We would go down to the front door with Dassie, prop the door open, and let him go for a long walk around the block <u>by himself</u>. He was also trained NOT to walk across any road without me, even though we were surrounded by four very heavy traffic roads in Burwood, a central Western suburb of Sydney, about 7 miles from downtown city. From our kitchen and lounge-room balcony we overlooked the large parking lot of Westfield and could see a grand view across the city. The traffic was constantly congested, yet Dassie would stand with me at the crossing and wait until the "WALK" light turned green before we would run across the road together. He would look up at me and wait until I said. "GO!", or would go when the light changed to green.

Since I explained that Dassie slept on or in my bed, I knew when to let him out in the mornings.

After Linda & I were married on 20th August, 1982, and flew to California for what turned out to be a year on our first trip, my mother had difficulty going up and down the stairs to let Dassie in and out, because someone usually took the prop from the front door, so my sister, Dawn and her husband, David took Dassie to live with them in their home by the sea at Maroubra. They had other dogs as well.

 I had spent my last hour in my apartment calming down my agitated Dassie who was shaking and anxious because he knew I was leaving him behind. He was 9 yrs old then, and lived his last 5-6 years with Dawn & David

GOD ALERTS ME TO DANGER IN AUSTRALIA

While we were in California the first part of 1983, I was awakened by God in the still of the night at about 2 am to PRAY and plead the blood of Jesus over Dassie, which I did intently. This came very clearly and I prayed for some time before going back to sleep.

Upon our return to Australia in September, 1983, we were told by my sister, Dawn, that Dassie usually went out for walks by himself each night. One evening he was attacked by a pack of wild dogs that lived in the mangroves behind their home, that was in the last street in the housing development across from the bush where some aborigines lived with these dogs. The dogs had ripped Dassie's rear end viciously and had come home bleeding profusely. He also had his head and ears attacked. The vet had to fight to save his life.

After Dassie recovered, he would not go out by himself again. At <u>precisely</u> 7 pm EVERY NIGHT Dassie would stand in the kitchen as Dawn washed the dishes, and look up at his leash and bark. We watched him do this when we were visiting. David walked him each night from that time, even though they had a decent sized back yard that was fenced.

Their younger daughter, my niece, Tracey, had another dog, a female boxer, that she <u>kept</u> in her parent's yard during the day. **She gave birth to a single pup, that looked like a boxe**r, but Dassie was also kept in the same yard. A 14-yr-old Dachshund male. HMMMN!

Very interesting.

A Horse friend, yet

Dassie had a close friend when I drove up to Dora Creek, near Morrisset, on the rail line to Newcastle, about 60 miles North of Sydney. That was where my sister had a weekender cottage built, only three houses from the main rail line from Sydney. The house next door had a horse in their back yard, and loved to run with Dassie. He would come to their side gate when we drove up and look for Dassie, who would get excited as well. They would allow Dassie to play with their horse.

Robbie also visited a home with horses, but they were both unfriendly to any dogs, even the ones on their land.

We have 3 big dogs next to our house and Robbie would snarl and bark at them on the other side of a long cyclone fence in a daily game. "Go, Tell them, Robbie," I would say, and he would run to the fence barking. It was a game to them too, for they are quiet dogs.

Our local banks like customer's dogs, too

Robbie always looked forward to the treats at the Union Bank office in Felton, as well as the Liberty Bank in Boulder Creek, and Washington Mutual Bank (Now CHASE) in Scotts Valley, and he was ever alert wanting to go inside when they were closed when I used their ATM's at night. **He would also love to rub his back on the carpet or soft grass, turning his upside down head from side to side, as he rubbed his back against the grass or carpet. We only have wooden floors upstairs at home and it was fun to hear Robbie running along the floor above us, when the door was opened for him.** We have sound board in our walls and ceiling and Robbie walked and ran heavily. I regret never having taken his photo when he did those funny things. His expression was in both his eyes and ears, that flopped back, when running, or sad, or when chastised, and propped forward when looking for food while people ate, or when he was very happy.

Unlike my last dachshund, Robbie would not sleep on his back, but stretched right out on one side or the other, and when he jumped onto his bed, he always headed for the right side and then turned his body to lie to the left at first, then would later move around and lie with his head to the right arm of the chair. When asleep on the floor he would lie straight out on his stomach, unless he had gone for a run and would then lie on one side, and that showed us he was very tired.

He chased the food sources at home, running to the refrigerator every time we opened it, or to the microwave whenever we heated anything up, but we warned the others not to feed Robbie anything but fruit or veges. **After we always fed him at 9:00 am & 5:00 p.m.** he went outside then upstairs knowing when Holly or her boarder ate (at irregular times and late at night), and whenever I found him on the back patio deck outside the rear door, Robbie would sheepishly walk over to me, as I stood beside him on the ground, and come and nudge my face and lick me through the rails, and immediately walk back downstairs. It was uncanny how he **always knew the TIME of his daily feeding**, except the switches at Daylight Savings, that had him looking for a meal an hour out. It was amazing how accurate his feeding clock was. Usually almost right on time he would look up and we would know it was feed time. Or he would pick up his feed dish and tip it upside down, or just look up and bark once.

He never whined or begged, but just sat there and stared. We tried not to feed him at our table and most of the times he would just sit under the table and wait in case something dropped. Many times when I would call him and ask, "Hungry, Robbie?" To which he would wag his tail fast, shaking his whole body in anticipation. He was very responsive.

Run, don't walk

We have no fences on the other three sides of the property, and Robbie would walk outside and around the land, but never on our road to the cul-de-sac where we live. He had very good car sense, even though there is little traffic. He loved to walk and run ahead of me. He usually stood still if I called out, **"STAY, ROBBIE!"** Looking back to see if I was close, he would then run some more until I said it was time to go back.

Once he lost me around the streets of Mt. Hermon and one of the staff recognized Robbie and tried to catch him, but he ran too fast. He heard my calling his name, but did not wait but ran all the way back to the Post Office, where I found him waiting, on the ramp outside the door& close to the car.

At the daily pick up of my mail, he would always come in with me (to collect his pay?) and then wait at the end of the ramp for me to put the mail inside our car, then RUN up the pathway towards the pool and open field area. He sure loved to run, even when he became obese or ill. Thank God we were able to get his weight down very easily.

He did not always recognize our car, and if a car door was opened outside our house by a guest, it was an invitation for Robbie to jump inside. He loved riding in cars. He had his favorite place to lie down in our cars, with his head on the door arm rest on the rear passenger seat, but did not like anything else laying on his seat. **Whenever we had to leave him in our car he always moved into the front driver's seat which is my seat most of the time.** He would stand up on the dash with his front legs looking where we were going whenever we approached a familiar place or within 1 mile from home, when he sat in the passenger seat in front. And when in the back after resting where he laid out with his head on the passenger side armrest if no-one else was sitting in the back, but if a person sat beside him he would snuggle up to them and put his head upon their thigh. If in the back, he would place one front leg on the top of either bucket seat and look between us, licking either person if they spoke to him. As I said previously, Robbie did not like any luggage or packages sharing his seat, as they sometimes fell on him as we went around a corner. Once we came home with the car filled with balloons, and I mean FILLED, so I could not see through the rear vision mirror. Robbie was not pleased at all and was glad to get out of the car at home.

Whenever we drove towards Placerville on Highway 50 he would get up, looking out and give a very slight wimper about 5-7 miles before our son's home where Robbie was living for his first 4 years. The only other times he would do this is when he was in the car for a long period and telling us he had to go to the bathroom. He never disgraced himself other than marking our daughter's carpet ONCE in a territorial bid against their dog. Every other time he would go to their kitchen door and look out or bark. He stayed with them a few times when we had to leave him overnight, and was extremely well-behaved. Robin & DREW were blessed by him with their golden retriever happy to see him visit.

SAMANTHA, DREW & ROBIN'S DOG, WAS ROBBIE'S FRIEND

ANOTHER FRIEND WITH ROBBIE. (They both speak German???)

Robbie with OLIVIA

(My Linda's middle name, too, as well as her mother's name)

LINDA HOLDING BRUTUS BUCKEYE, A CHOCOLATE MINIATURE WE MET IN BRANSON, MISSOURI, IN MAY 2009

WHO? ME?

ROBBIE POSED FOR HIS PHOTOS.

Robbie goes to HOLLYWOOD

When we drove down to stay in one of our Australian producer's friend's mate's house in Hollywood to do Movie interviews over a period of 6 weeks in the Summer of 2005, our friend paid for the renewing of the air conditioning in our 19 year old Ford LTD sedan (which according to one of our mechanics means <u>F</u>ound <u>O</u>n the <u>R</u>oad <u>D</u>ead or <u>F</u>ix <u>O</u>r <u>R</u>epair <u>D</u>aily) for otherwise we could not have gone down to pick him and his dad up at Los Angeles Airport and stay in that oppressive heat through August/ September. We could not have even survived the trip down it was so humid.

Of course we had to take Robbie with us as he would have thought we had abandoned him if we left him at home in our long absence. There was just enough space for Robbie to squeeze into his regular spot beside all the luggage. Praise God that the owner was there to meet us when we arrived and soon after we arrived, we drove him to the airport as he conducted his regular business overseas. We had asked about Robbie coming down and staying in his house with us and thankfully he approved. David had replaced the Air Conditioning in his home in his absence while we were there as well. It was a really hot Summer in 2005.

Our Aussie mate just had to go to both Universal Studios and Disneyland, so we had to leave Robbie in the house by himself all day and night twice. I am sure he did understand. But otherwise he behaved himself accordingly, with early morning walks around the streets hoping to meet any celebrity. Alas he did get filmed, but no Robbie contract was offered him while he was there hoping to get discovered. We began to get our bearings easily and the location was great for about every freeway surrounding the house, and with my professional driving experience that came in handy to find our way around.

We did get two important interviews on film, one with Barbara Eden, that came about after much perseverance and in time for her annual Labradoodle gathering near Malibu where Robbie would have been quite comfortable surrounded by about 100 of these lovely dogs of all sizes as they romped around a large tree covered bush-style, open space for a huge picnic. Unfortunately we believed it prudent to have Robbie stay home with Linda while we took Victor's elderly father instead. I had to apologize to him after we returned as he sniffed me and knew I had preferred those dogs to his going with me.

Do you see the genie bottle?

Labradoodles were bred in Australia as an experiment with a Poodle cross with a Labrador for a Hypoallergenic, non-shedding variety of quiet, intelligent guide dogs and pets for disabled persons who could not use the regular type. Barbara has a medium sized brown male called Djin Djin after her "Jeannie" T.V. show. Barbara had invited us along prior to granting Victor an interview the following Monday in her beautiful home in Beverly Hills.

AT HOME,

We have dirt and hard clay on the ground at the back, and redwood leaves constantly falling around our house. Robbie made two trails through the gravel and leaves, like a "Y", with one trail to the rear cottage, and the other side going to the back porch. If the front side French doors were not locked, Robbie would push one open to go inside, leaving it wide open.

People were often surprised at the power of Robbie's nose and snout in his pushing open heavy doors when he wanted to go outside.

Robbie and Water don't mix

Robbie HATED getting his feet wet, or rainy days, and we live in the WETTEST part of the Santa Cruz mountains, with upwards of 60 inches per month in severe Winters. So in the morning he would go to the door, looking outside several times until he HAD to go out. The word BATH was not a happy one, but Robbie was obedient, and when I took off his collar, he knew what was coming next, and walked around to the front door and into the front bathroom with me as I put my towel on the hook. After I had finished my shower, I would call out, "O.K. Robbie, its your turn now" he would come to the edge of the tub, and move his front legs from side to side before standing up on the tub and waiting for me to lift up his rear legs and put him inside. Then he would love to walk to the other end of the bathtub and under the warm / hot shower. He liked the hot water actually. When finished rinsing he would jump out, by himself and I would put one towel onto the floor and wipe him down and then use a hair dryer as he stood there.

His ears were hard to dry and very sensitive. Did NOT like anyone touching them. As I opened the bathroom door, Robbie would RUN out and roll on the front rug in the living room, and run downstairs with me, where I put another towel over him as he jumped up onto his bed. His ears seemed to be the last part of him that dried.

My second Dachshund, Dassie, loved to swim in water, even as I went fishing some days, even jumping out of the boat when we were waiting for a fish to bite. But NOT our ROBBIE. NO WAY he would ever go in the surf if running along a beach with me, or anything remotely wet. All dogs have their own personalities. He was very careful when walking besides the "big bath", the swimming pools.

Don't cross me!

He had many different expressions and you just KNEW what he wanted by the way he looked at you. He was a very loving dog, and sometimes he would just walk around our bed and stand up and want you to pat him, before going back and laying down again. As long as he was with someone he was happy. One day I was leaving for work, and could not take Robbie with me that day, no one else was home, and I thought Linda and Holly were coming home in an hour or less, and LOCKED HIM INSIDE.

Big mistake!

Unfortunately, I called into our daughter's home in Los Gatos after work and Linda was still there at 8 pm. When we came home at about 9 pm. Robbie had been locked in for over 9 hours, and no dinner. Poor little boy was not amused. He had slept in his bed for probably the whole time, and was very hungry when we came home, but held his bladder the whole time as well.

After that treatment, he was so insecure with me for a time that every time Linda went upstairs he immediately took off with her and would NOT stay with me inside our room. It took many, many weeks to get his trust and confidence back, even though he always went to work with me at every opportunity. After many weeks he relaxed himself again and decided that he would forgive me after all. But it was not easy for him for a long, long time.

DOGS & MUSIC, other sounds

Karl was a singing dachshund, howling along with me as we sang together, whereas both Dassie and Robbie hadn't the slightest interest in howling, and **Robbie would not care if all the sirens screamed past us along the highway #9 route and ALL the neighborhood dogs howled together, he would totally ignore them.** We live about halfway between two fire stations along Highway #9, so there were always sirens in close proximity to our home, which is ½ mile from that Highway, but much closer as the crows fly. He loved classical music, especially BACH and OFFENBACH.

Dogs do not like thunderstorms and we were blessed in that we live in the Santa Cruz Mountains and for as long as we have lived here on a crest of the hill amongst the redwood trees none of the storms ever come close to us, stopping short of about half a mile away every time. No lightning has ever come down in our vicinity for the past 17 years. The terrain has a built in protection somehow. But we have been caught in several storms whilst driving together, and Robbie would look at me intently whenever a flash of lightning and thunder came close to our car.

RUN, ROBBIE, RUN

THE WHOLE TIME HE WAS WITH US, FOR ALMOST TWELVE YEARS, ROBBIE WALKED A LOT, BUT LOVED TO RUN AND RUN, NEVER BY HIMSELF, BUT **ALWAYS RUNNING WITH SOMEONE**. THE ONLY TIMES WE PUT HIM ON A LEASH WERE WHEN WALKING THE STREETS OF SAN FRANCISCO ON OUR FREQUENT VISITS AND ONCE DOWN PACIFIC AVENUE, SANTA CRUZ <u>WHEN WE PRAYER WALKED DOWNTOWN SANTA CRUZ TOGETHER</u>.

HE EVEN TRIED TO RUN THE DAY BEFORE I TOOK HIM TO THE VET, BECAUSE HE WAS HAVING A HARD TIME BREATHING, BUT ONLY OVER THE LAST WEEK OF HIS LIFE. WE WALKED FROM THE POST OFFICE TO THE POOL AT MT HERMON, AND HE RAN DOWN THERE AND PART OF THE WAY BACK UNTIL HE HAD TO STOP. I NOTICED THAT HE WAS SLOWING DOWN OVER THE PAST MONTH, AND THAT ALL WAS NOT THE SAME, AFTER ALL ROBBIE WOULD BE 16 YEARS OLD NEXT MONTH.(NOVEMBER,2007) WE HAD TO LIFT HIS BACK END UP ONTO HIS BED AND INTO THE CAR MOST OF THE TIME, BUT HE STILL JUMPED UP BY HIMSELF AS WELL.

ROBBIE WOULD STAY IN A CAR ALL DAY IF WE ALLOWED HIM

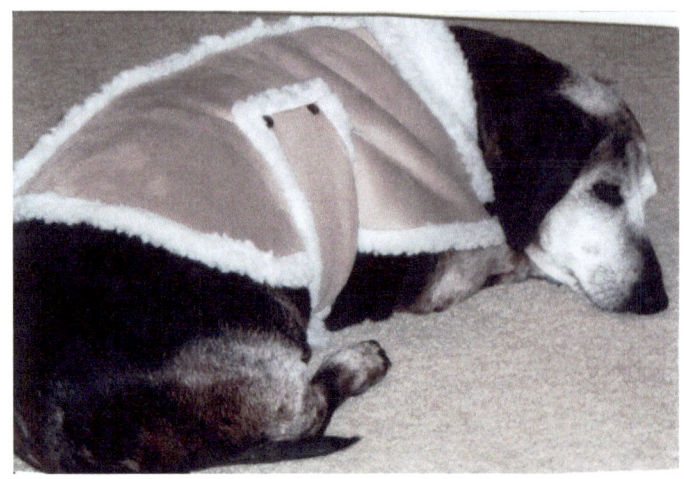

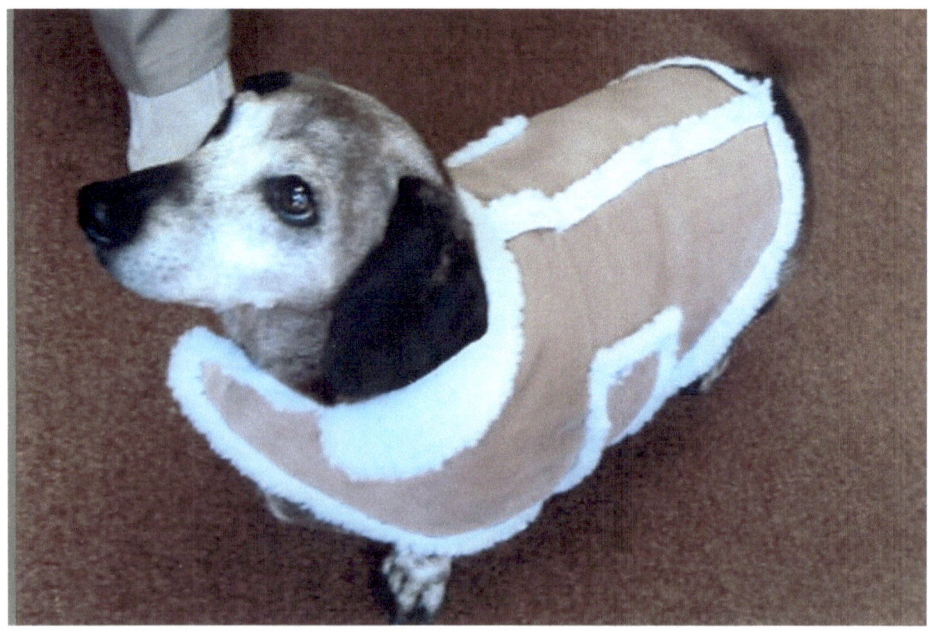

ROBBIE FELT THE CHILL OF WINTERS & LOVED HIS COAT

ROBBIE'S FINAL NIGHT WITH US

That night he labored in his breathing and we were very concerned, The vet had him for X-Rays Thursday and said his heart murmur had doubled to a 4 from a 2 since July, and that he needed complete rest and his heart was very enlarged and fluid was on both lungs. He was o.k. for the next 2 days, but refused his food at breakfast on Sat and Sun, but ate at night. This was NOT our Robbie who ate like a vacuum cleaner.

When we came home the final Sunday night @ 9:30 p.m. Robbie was sleeping soundly on Holly's armchair when I awakened him by just touching an ear. He jumped down and walked downstairs with us. I lifted him onto his bed, but he was very short in his breathing and came down soon after and tried to sleep on the floor, moving around several times, **waking me up at 3 am and from 4 am I was with him Monday morning.** When I went upstairs to the bathroom, **I came back at 6:40 am and could not find him.** So, I went outside in the darkness to search for him with a flashlight, and located Robbie on the back porch, **UP 5 STEPS,** lying there, shivering. He had also gone out for a very small bowel movement, because he had hardly eaten over the weekend. His last meal was part of a can of tuna that Grandma Holly had given him. I carried up to his bed and covered him up, but we knew we could do no more for him, as he was struggling to breathe. <u>We had prayer for him ever since we knew the problem.</u> At **7:15** am he stopped struggling and laid his head back on the pillow and breathed very slightly in peace, and I put my hand on his neck and my head on his chest to listen to his heart beat for another few heartbeats and then it stopped. We have lost a very dear family friend.

He had no back or leg problems, no pain, or loss of senses, all his other organs were in perfect condition, his body temperature was normal, it was just God's Time for Robbie to go.

His faithfulness and loyalty and obedience were amazing. He would go to anyone that I told him to, **licking any open flesh, not covered by clothes.** His sight, hearing and smell were still vivid and alive up to the end. He just slowed down a little, but the strength of this little dog was constantly shown. **He would climb up stairs or steps two at a time with his very short legs. He did have a very big heart.**

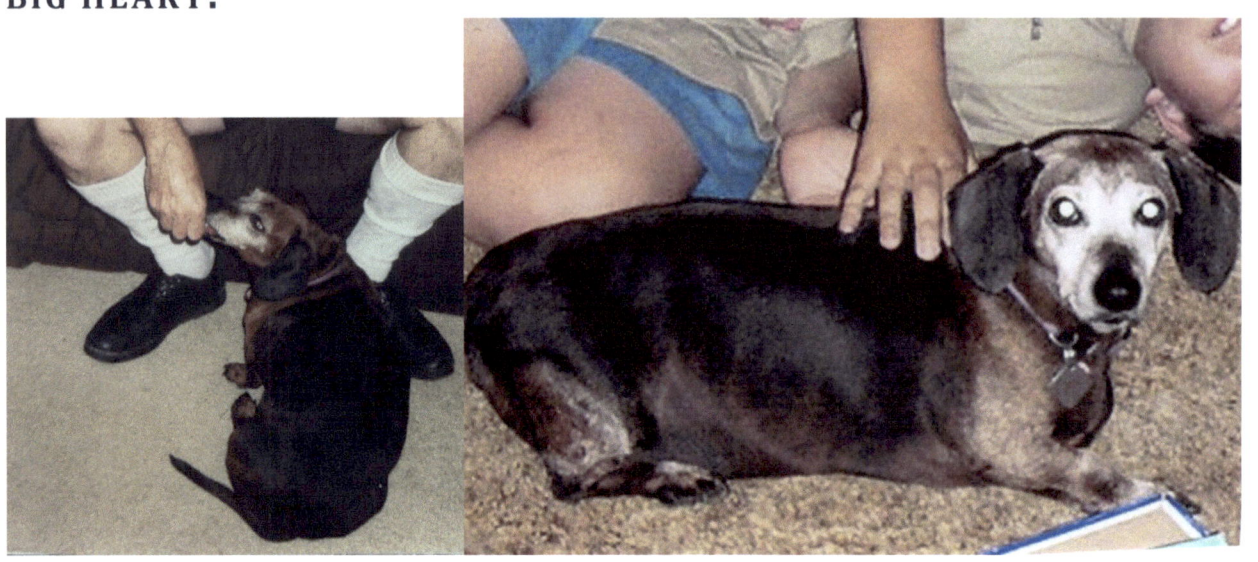

We knew he was <u>suddenly</u> getting old when he needed assistance to get up onto his bed. He would lean up, placing his front legs on the pillow and turn around to ask us to lift his rear end up and then climb up with our lift. It was the same in the car, which he loved to stay in, even for hours, if we went somewhere that he could not go inside with us. But I either did not want to accept it or failed to fully recognize that something was wrong in the past couple of months. **He was ALWAYS FULLY OBEDIENT until about 1-2 months before he died. He was trying to tell us he was not right.** I did not realize that he was starting to slip away and that he was making a slight noise, like snoring, while sleeping, at times, and then he would start panting slowly in the back seat when it was not hot in the car. **But it was not really noticeable until the last few days.**

I know he went in God's timing, as his heart murmur had doubled in the last 3 months, his heart was enlarged and he had fluid in both lungs and we had prayed fervently against the illnesses hoping for another healing miracle against all odds.

He looked up to us for help at the end, and there was nothing else we could do except release Robbie into God's hands, We are very thankful that he did not have pain or suffering other than difficulty in breathing for a few short days. **He must have known as he went off his food completely over the final 2 days, having only part of a can of tuna as his final meal.**

It is just so hard to live without Robbie. I was wondering what he was thinking as he drifted away, what memories he was reliving. He was such a loving animal. He would sometimes just sit or lie there <u>looking intently at us</u>.

I asked God "Why now? And will I see Robbie again in Heaven?"

And He answered me with, ***"Hounds of Heaven"*- God said, *"How do you know that Robbie isn't one of these that you prayed for over the years?"*** I remember praying that God would send the Hounds of Heaven to corner someone into turning to Him for help when they were avoiding Him, or in denial of a need to seek Him.

Also, on our younger daughter, Christina's, birthday in December, 2007 the Lord gave my wife, Linda a word about Robbie for me:

> *"See Robbie run in the sun of the rest of his life. Well, that sun has turned into MY SON, who is shining upon Robbie, Phillip."*

Then I attended a memorial service about 2 months later for a very kind man I knew who had passed into Glory and his widow remembered and asked after Robbie. When I told her what happened she said, *"Robbie is waiting for you in your mansion in heaven"*

(The NEW JERUSALEM that is being prepared for return to a new Earth after YESHUA COMES BACK TO REIGN as KING of KINGS.)"

Everyone loved that special dog. When I wrote about his dying, I received dozens of e-mails from those who knew him. I have included many of them at the end of this little book

HAVING OUR SECURITY PHOTO TAKEN FOR VISA CARD

FROZEN ROBBIE SENT BY FEDEX TO BE PROCESSED:

PHILLIP & LINDA LEMKIN   Phone: Cell: 1 831 212 6855

P.O. BOX 481

MT. HERMON, CA 95041   lustylamb888@juno.com

Mon, 29th October, 2007

Al's Taxidermy   1 760 961 2434   AL BACON

26080 Rancho Street,   CELL   1 760 964 8347

APPLE VALLEY, CA 92308

Dear Al,

Further to our phone call of last week, we enclose our pet dachshund, ROBBIE for Freeze-Drying as we discussed. Please have him lying straight with his head lifted up as in the enclosed photo. (25 lbs weight)

Our check for $XXXX   is also enclosed in full payment.

Thank you for your kindly efforts.

Please advise when Robbie is ready to come home.

Sincerely,

Phillip & Linda

FEDEX 30.74 lbs

MON 29th Oct,07 2 DAYS @ $64.00 4 pm.   To arrive by Weds 31st Oct 4 pm. Apple Valley, Ca

```
Our records indicate that the following shipment has been delivered:
Ship (P/U) date:              Oct 29, 2007
Delivery date:                Oct 31, 2007 12:57 PM
Sign for by:                  A.BACON
Delivered to:                 Residence
Service type:                 FedEx 2Day
```

ROBBIE back from APPLE VALLEY, CA

It took 3 months to complete the process.

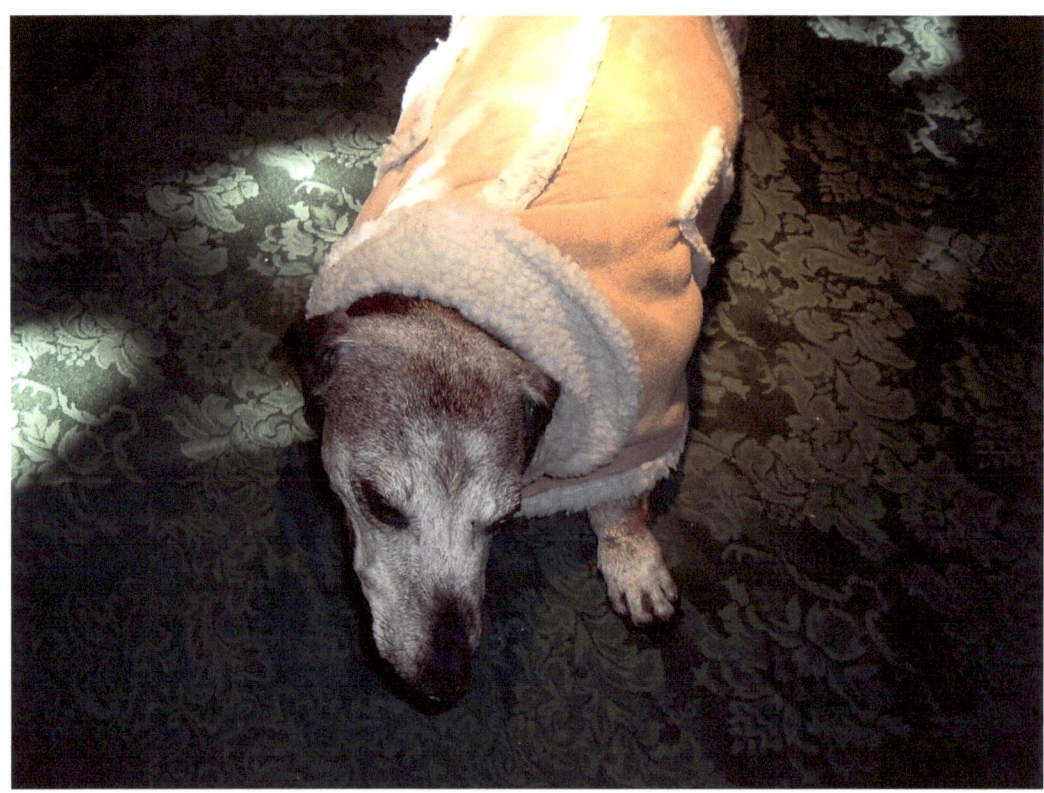

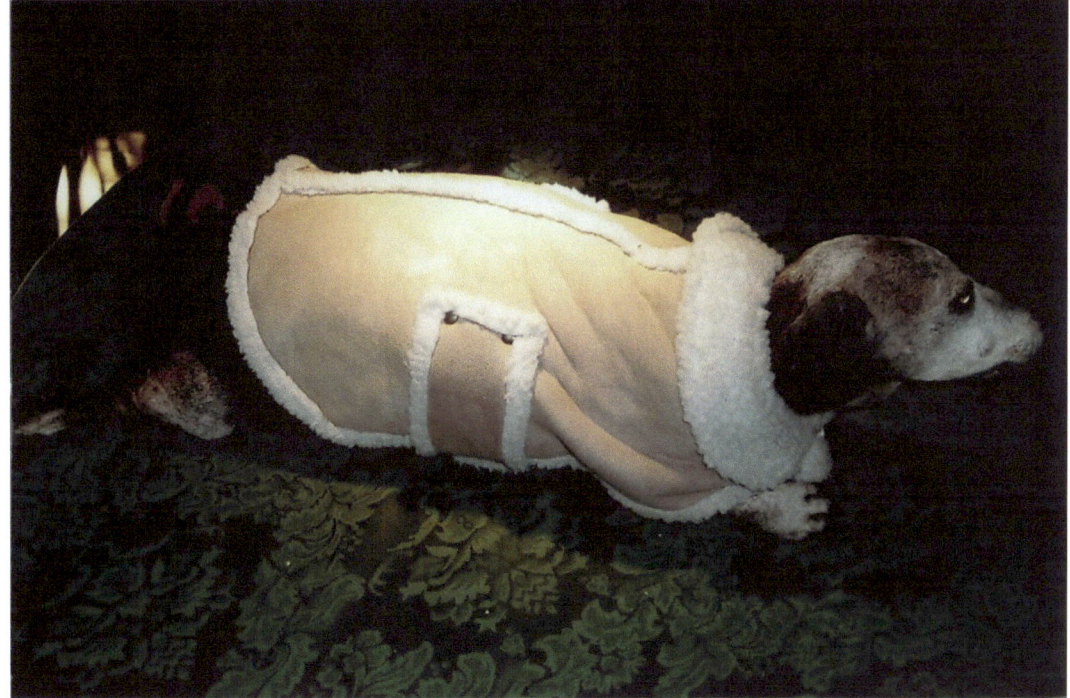

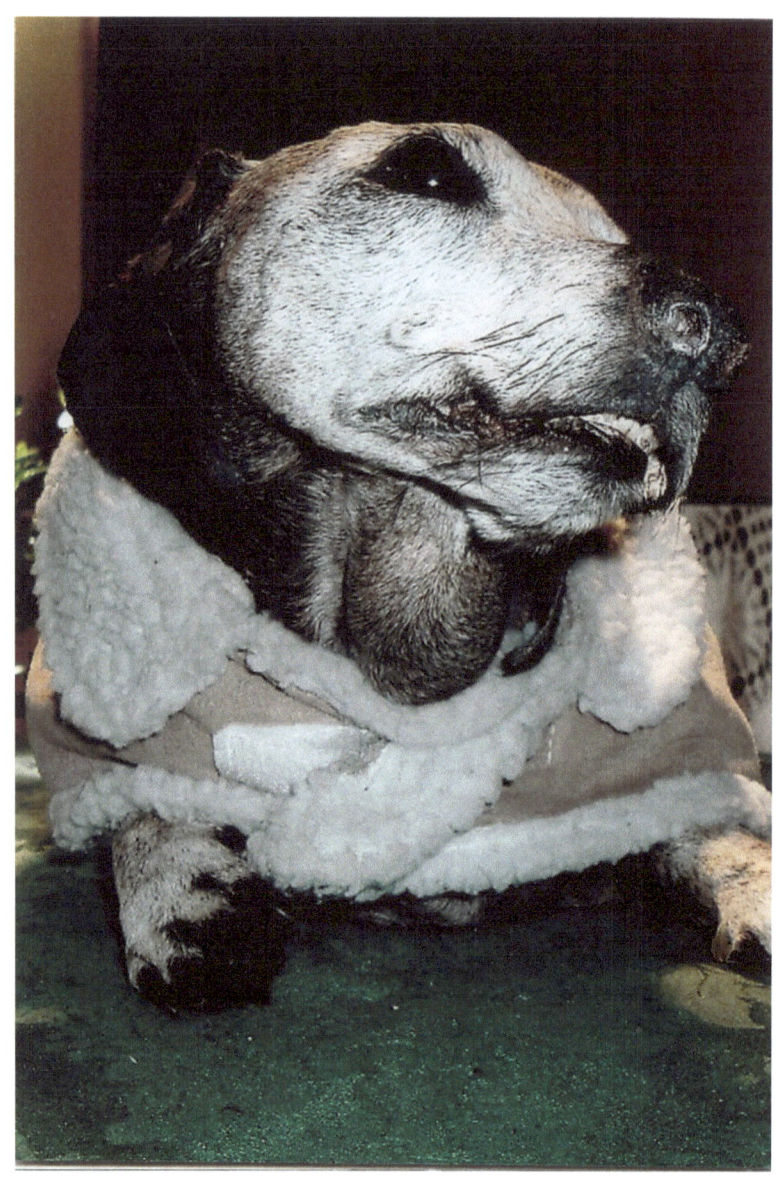

ROBBIE as he is now.

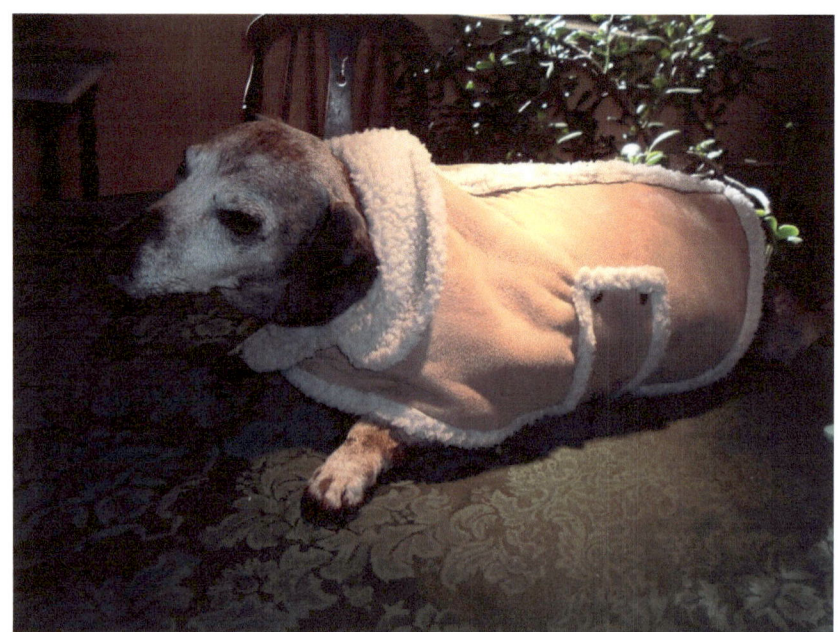

ROBBIE LEMKIN.   1st NOV,1991 – 22nd OCT 2007

OBITUARY for our Robbie   22nd October, 2007

Dear friends,

Last week we had to take Robbie to the vet again- he had a rough year this year- bitten by a raccoon and recovered quickly among other issues. His X-rays showed an enlarged heart and fluid on both lungs. I took him for his last walk on Weds, and he ran for a while but was very slow coming back to the car, Thurs the vet said no more walks. He responded to the medication until Sunday night when he again had very labored breathing after we came come late. He was looking to us for help and was moving across the bedroom floor choosing to sleep beside our bed and I was praying with him since about 4 am today after we noticed he was worse. He refused his breakfast twice and was fasting over the weekend, but ate later on He also refused his medication last night and also this morning..

At 6:40 am he walked outside and up 5 steps to the back door when I was upstairs, probably looking for me, and I carried him back down to his bed and stayed with him until he stopped breathing at 7:15 this morning, a couple of minutes after he stopped the laboring, just resting his head quietly as I petted and loved him. I checked his pulse just before and after he died.

Robbie came here several times before we took him from our son's house in Placerville after he bit a UPS driver the day before, when he was 4, so we had him here with us in our bedroom for almost 12 years. Robbie was the third dachshund I have had, and by far the most intelligent and loving. He would have been sixteen (102 in human years, it has been said)) in nine days.

Many people will miss him. He gave us very much joy and company. He went to more churches than most people ever visit, including Prayer for him at Redwood last Thursday night. He was prayed for by many people over the years. God gave Robbie DOUBLE his life when he probably should have died in 1999 with an interior blockage that was dissolved by the Lord after our anointing & intense prayer in front of the vets in Angels Camp,CA. and we took him home intact (after an operation to search out the problem the night before and 3 days in intensive care on an I.V. drip, and multiple X-Rays over 48 hours.

THEY FOUND NOTHING and said his organs were in perfect condition.

We praise God for the years he gave us, and for so little suffering at the end. We will miss Robbie so much.

I rest in His Presence, for Jesus alone can ease our grief.

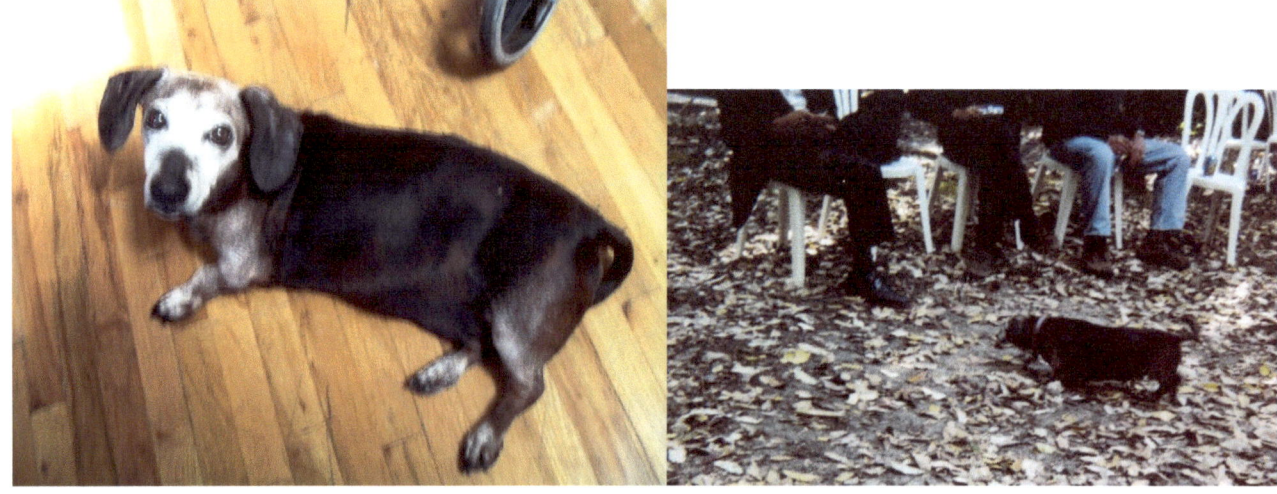

Robbie with Linda & younger daughter, Christina

CONDOLENCES FROM E-MAIL RESPONSES TO ROBBIE'S PASSING

Sent: Monday, October 22, 2007 9:01:19 AM
Subject: **WE LOST ROBBIE THIS MORNING**

I'm sorry to hear about Robbie. I knew he meant so much to you.

Love,

Beverly and Dan

Shalom, my friends; I am blessed to hear of how much Robbie blessed and comforted you both during his time with you. Miracles and more..that's quite a statement for for most people to have about their special pet...I pray the comfort, joy, and shalom of YHVH upon you both....and I look forward to the next time together.

Brother DON FINEGAN

JEFF & TATIANA MILWEE
: Wed, Oct 24, 2007
Dear Guys,
We will miss Robbie, too! We enjoyed his times of him running around during the Bible studies at church and at Charles' place. We share your heart-felt sorrow. We know what it's like to lose a pet. Best wishes...
        Jeff and Tatiana

Philip and Linda,
We send our regards and love. Robbie was special and we know what such loss feels like. He will always be in your hearts as we know you already know. I enjoyed him a lot. Our prayers and thoughts are with you at this moment of sadness, stay in Gods love.

       Dayne and Rik

Dear Phillip and Linda

When my beloved pet named Bear died, it was as though my own flesh and blood had passed away. I found her one morning out on the street. There was not a mark on her. Her beautiful thick black fur was like it had always been. The pain was unbearable. **Soon after when we were at a Family Worship Center service, Pastor Drake gave a prophetic word that I would see her again.**

For those that God loves, he does special things. Many things are not be promised to all, but nonetheless, are given to some. **You are both very special people. God's favor rests upon you. He has chosen you to a peculiar calling that few can even fathom.**

Not all are taken from this earth as Elijah, not all are called the friend of God, not all will sit on twelve thrones judging the tribes of Israel, and not all will ever again see their beloved pet. **You, however, are not grouped with the many, but instead with the few. He is no respecter of persons. I am sure you will see Robbie again.**

Love and prayers

    Wayne and Margaret

RESPONSE TO: Wayne and Margaret SMITH,

Thank you so much for your kindly, encouraging words.

They mean so much to us, now that we lost such a good friend.

We BELIEVED GOD for his healing. I even prayed for his resurrection. Many others prayed with us for Robbie. I cannot stop crying, his loss just tears me up.

I am writing a book of "MEMORIES OF THE ROBBIE DOG" trying to recall everything that blessed us so much over the past 12 years.

We took him almost everywhere with us, into many, many churches, and I have received some fabulous replies already to the letter that I sent you.

Not even with the other 2 Dachshunds did I find such a sensitive, obedient and faithful dog with such a sense of the Spirit realm. He looked at us with depth, facing our bed from his raised padded wide chair. God blessed him with extremely good health until it was time to take him. He only had a hard time breathing for 6 days, even running with me the day befiore we took him to the vet last Thursday for the X-Rays and checkup. His expressions changed with his feelings. We have lots of photos but no videos.

We are thankful to Jesus because we know He has plans to SEND US OUT and we could no longer leave him with Linda's Mother, HOLLY, as she is almost 90 and had big problems getting him into her car on Sunday. He was fading fast. Praise the Lord for His Mercy endures FOREVER.

Sorry about this.......... as a animal lover I can not even imagine......may the little dog wait for you till it is your turn.. The Lord has His living creatures..

> *Lord let your Holy Anointing breath LIFE to this beloved of the Lord even NOW in Jesus Name.*
>
> *A multiplication on their lives!*
>
> **CHARIOTS OF FIRE MINISTRIES**
> Shani

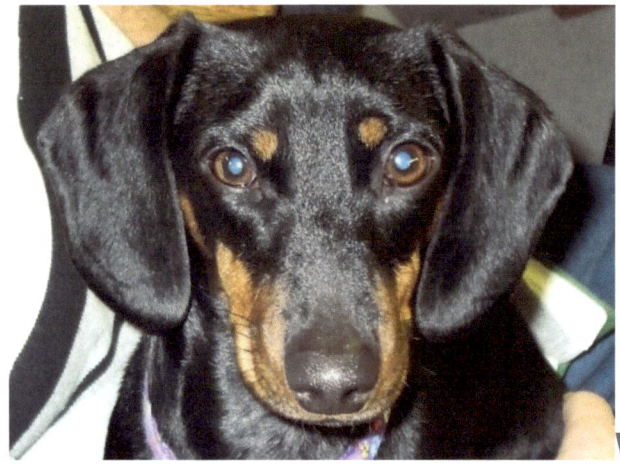

WOLFIE TENNESEN

Our hearts and prayers are with you, Phil and Linda... we all loved Robbie, and will miss him. He was a blessing to us all -- we, like you, rest in the God of all comfort -- II Cor. 1. I forwarded your note and pictures to David & Char Short, as they would want to know.

> God bless you all,
>
> Pastor Dick Tennesen (WHO NOW HAS TWO "WEENIES")
>
> *Also,*
>
> Dear Linda and Phil, Hi, Phil -- meditate on these, from Berit Kjos: Dick T.

We suffer now, but... OUR SUFFERING WILL END

Therefore you now have sorrow; but I will see you again and your heart will rejoice, and your joy no one will take from you. (John 16:22)

WHAT THE BIBLE SAYS

The earth will pass away. Rev 21:1-4, 1 Jn 2:15-17

We are only a vapor that appears for a little while and then vanishes. James 4:13-17, Ps 39:5-7

The things we see now (this world) are temporary, while the things we do not see are eternal. 2 Cor 4:16-18

In the world we *will* have trouble, but take heart because He has overcome the world. Jn 16:33

Life is like childbirth – pain while on earth turns to joy when we see Jesus. Jn 16:20-22

The suffering of this present earth are not worthy to be compared with the future glory. Rom 8:15-26

After we suffer, God will restore us and make us strong, firm and steadfast. 1 Peter 5:8-11

When suffering, our confidence of a better and enduring possession in heaven will be richly rewarded. Heb 10:34-39

We are suffering now for the kingdom of God. 2 Thes 1:5-7

We groan waiting for our adoption. Romans 8:23-25

We will be glad with exceeding joy (if we suffered for Him). 1 Pet 4:12-15

REASONS FOR OUR SUFFERING

We suffer now so that our faith, of greater worth than gold, may be proved genuine and result in praise, glory and honor. 1 Peter 1:3-9

Sorrow produces repentance leading to salvation. It also produces other godly characteristics. 2 Cor 7:9-11

Ultimately, if we partake in Christ's suffering, our suffering will bring exceeding joy. 1 Pet 4:12-15

Suffering occurs so that we might trust in God and not ourselves. *2 Co 1:8-11*

Suffering keeps us humble and lets God's strength work in us. *2 Cor 12:7-10*

We suffer so that we can comfort others. *2 Cor 1:3-7*

Our current light affliction is working for us a more eternal weight of glory. *2 Cor 4:16-18*

God's discipline here is painful, but it reaps later rewards. *Heb 12:7-11*

Our suffering now is evidence of the righteousness of God's judgment later when he takes vengeance justly. *2 Thes 1:4-10*

We are obligated to suffer for Christ. *Php 1:29-30*

We are promised to suffer persecution. *2 Tim 3:12-13*

OUR PROPER RESPONSE

We should be patient for the Lord's return (like a farmer waits for rain), and we should strengthen and stabilize our hearts for the Lord's return. *James 5:7-11*

We should not lose heart while fixing our eyes on eternal things and knowing that the troubles we have are only momentary. *2 Cor 4:16-18*

We should be sober, diligent, resist the devil (steadfast in the faith), knowing that we are not alone in our sufferings. *1 Peter 5:8-11*

We should bear Jesus' reproach while we seek the city that is to come. *Heb 13:12-14*

We should be faithful during our suffering (even to death), and He will give us life. *Revelation 2:10*

Examples of patience: A farmer, the prophets and Job. In the end, the Lord is compassionate and merciful to those who trust Him. *James 5:7-11*

We should remember the suffering Jesus endured from others - and for us. *Heb 12:3* (See *Christ's Example*)

We are only a vapor that appears for a little while and then vanishes. *Ps 39:5-7*

These are only a few of more than fifty e-mails sent by those who knew Robbie

CONTACT: PHILLIP LEMKIN   aussiephil@Robbiedoggie.com

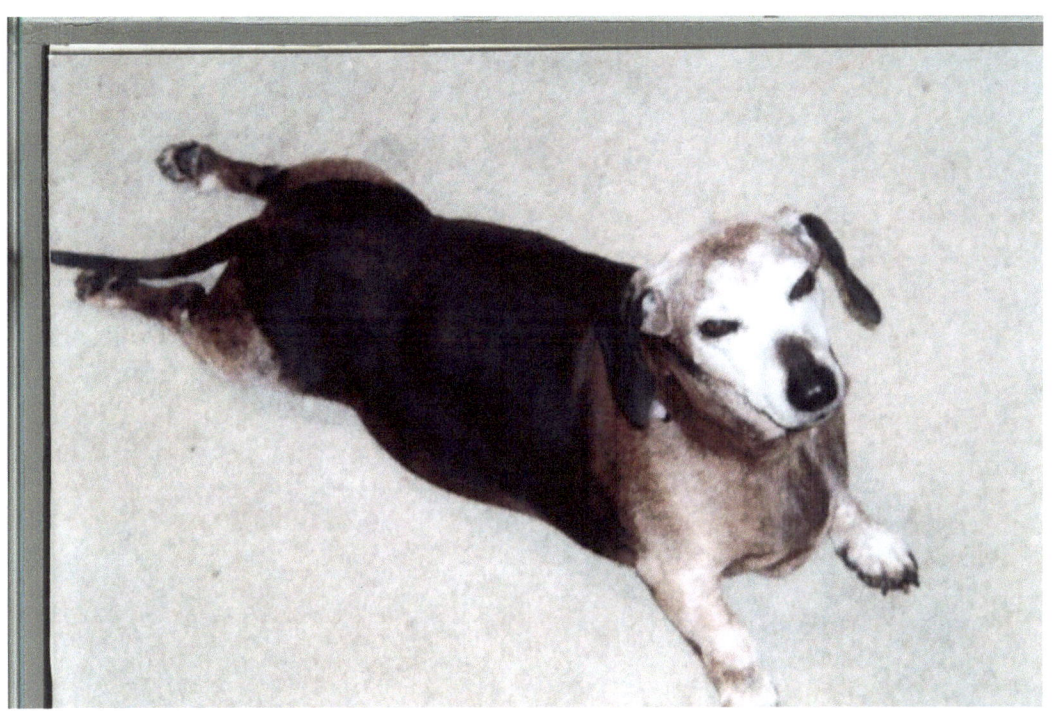

THIS PHOTO WAS TAKEN LONG BEFORE HE DIED, BUT IT IS AS IF HE POSED FOR HIS RETURN FROM

APPLE VALLEY, CA

SHOULD ANYONE HAVE A SPECIAL PRAYER REQUEST, I WILL BE GLAD TO SEEK JESUS' RESPONSE FOR YOU AS YOU PRAY IN AGREEMENT WITH ME (& ROBBIE) IN JESUS NAME.

aussiephil@Robbiedoggie.com

Jesus said that… **IF TWO or more AGREE** on Earth as touching anything that they shall ASK, it SHALL be done for them by MY FATHER which is in Heaven.

For where **TWO or THREE are gathered T OGETHER IN MY NAME**, there AM I in the MIDST of them.

(Matthew 18:18-19)

And, IF you ABIDE in ME, and MY WORDS ABIDE in you, you shall ASK what you will & it shall be done unto you

(John 15:7)

www.ingramcontent.com/pod-product-compliance
Lightning Source LLC
Chambersburg PA
CBHW041124300426
44113CB00002B/51